Charles Evans Hughes
and
American Democratic Statesmanship

Dexter Perkins

Charles Evans Hughes *and* American Democratic Statesmanship

GREENWOOD PRESS, PUBLISHERS
WESTPORT, CONNECTICUT

Library of Congress Cataloging in Publication Data

Perkins, Dexter, 1889-
Charles Evans Hughes and American democratic statesmanship.

Reprint of the ed. published by Little, Brown, Boston, in series: The Library of American biography.
Bibliography: p.
Includes index.
1. Hughes, Charles Evans, 1862-1945. 2. Statesmen --United States--Biography. 3. Judges--United States--Biography. 4. United States--Foreign relations--1921-1923. 5. United States--Politics and government--1901-1953. 6. United States. Supreme Court--Biography. I. Handlin, Oscar, 1915- II. Title. III. Series: Library of American biography.
E748.H88P4 1978] 973.91'092'4 [B] 78-5919
ISBN 0-313-20463-2 lib. bdg.

Reprinted by permission of Little, Brown and Company, Inc.

Reprinted in 1978 by Greenwood Press, Inc.,
51 Riverside Avenue, Westport, CT. 06880

Printed in the United States of America

10 9 8 7 6 5 4 3 2 1

To
M.G.

Contents

Editor's Preface

SINCE THE EIGHTEENTH CENTURY the connection between the practice of law and the operations of government has grown increasingly more intimate. As the state grew more complex, the amateur became ever less capable of managing its intricacies with competence. Lawyers have therefore taken a prominent part in political life, and the concepts derived from their profession have entered significantly and subtly into the assumptions of American statesmanship.

Yet the lawyer has always played an ambiguous role, and that has frequently influenced his practice as a politician. On the one hand, he is an officer of the court, and thus concerned, as is the court, with the abstract and impartial administration of justice. On the other hand, he represents the interests of his client, and his obligation is to further those interests to the utmost of his powers. In day-to-day practice, each practitioner resolves that conflict to the best of his ability. Only when he ascends the bench as judge, can the lawyer leave that conflict of duties behind him and dedicate himself entirely to the law as justice.

So, too, the lawyer who accepts elective or appointive office often confronts the necessity of choice between two obligations. On the one hand, he serves an abstract entity — the people of the state or of the nation. On the other hand, he finds himself acting as the spokesman of particular groups who wish the actions of the government bent to the service of their own interests. The politician who acts the role of statesman is one who is capable of resolving the conflicts between these two obligations.

The problem had already made itself clear in the nineteenth century. In modern America, it became more impelling still. The enormous growth in the power of government at all levels, the creation of sharply contending groups in an industrial society, and the extension of American interests beyond the continental borders of the United States called for adjustments few politicians were capable of making. To a significant degree, success in American politics thereafter depended on the ability to meet these challenges.

The life of Charles E. Hughes embraced all these problems. His career began as that of the successful lawyer, and the early part of his life was dedicated to the defense of the interests of the great corporations which were his clients. Then he was called into action in politics, distinguishing himself as governor of the State of New York. But his own conception of his role was still uncertain.

After his unsuccessful campaign for the Presidency in 1916, he came more clearly to understand the nature of statesmanship. As Secretary of State, and later as Chief Justice of the Supreme Court, he applied that understanding to the problems of foreign and domestic policy. In so doing, he contributed significantly to the practice of American statesmanship. His prolonged efforts to resolve the dilemmas of the lawyer throw meaningful light on the most critical problems of the twentieth century.

OSCAR HANDLIN

Author's Preface

It has been a great delight to me to write this little book. The major problem of politics is the problem of a just balance between conservatism and liberalism. While it would be too much to say that Charles Evans Hughes attained that balance to perfection, he surely represented in his strong will and clear mind the desire to see that balance attained. This I have tried to show.

In the preparation of this work I have had much assistance. I have profited from conversations with Judge Felix Frankfurter, the late Justice Owen J. Roberts, and John Lord O'Brian, all of whom have given me new insights into Hughes's character. I am deeply indebted to both Professor Paul Freund of the Harvard Law School and Judge Charles Wyzanski of the United States District Court for their reading of the chapters which deal with Hughes as judge, and I value highly their comment and criticism. My assistants at Cornell University, Murray Rosenthal, David A. Tiffany, and Lin Webster, have all performed important services in connection with the research necessary for this study. And it has been a special pleasure through my friendly association with Mrs. Chauncey Waddell to catch a glimpse of Hughes as seen by an affectionate and discerning daughter.

Professor Oscar Handlin of Harvard, the editor of this series (The Library of American Biography), has read the text with scrupulous care, and I have profited much from his suggestions.

I wish also to mention one other indebtedness — a great one. This is the sixth book of mine to which my secretary, Miss Marjorie Gilles, has given her intense interest, her meticulous attention to detail, and her thoughtful judgment. I therefore inscribe it to her.

DEXTER PERKINS

Cornell University
Ithaca, New York

Introduction

THE MOST IMPORTANT THING about Charles E. Hughes is certainty. The generalization is scarcely set down before it needs qualification. In the bosom of his family Hughes was often a prey to self-doubt; he was sensitive to criticism; and he was far too intelligent not to weigh both sides of important questions that arose in the course of his personal and professional life. Nonetheless, he gives us the impression of a man who knew what his scale of values was, who knew what he wanted and what he cared little for, what he believed and what he did not believe.

He was the son of very strong-minded parents. His father was a minister with positive views on the kingdom of heaven and the kingdom of sin. His mother was a devout and vigorous-minded woman with no nonsense about her. Both were the kind of people who sought to dominate, and might have succeeded in dominating, their only son. But it did not work out that way. At the age of six the boy had worked out the Charles E. Hughes plan of study for the guidance of his work and had persuaded his parents to permit him to study at home instead of going to school. At the age of fourteen, once again knowing what he wanted (freedom from parental supervision), he entered Madison (now Colgate) University. After two years, desiring a broader and freer atmosphere, he transferred to Brown. By this time he was clear (contrary to the views of his parents) that card playing was not immoral, that smoking was an innocent amusement, and that even a glass of beer was no certain passport to damnation. His religious views, too, were changing, and by the end of his college course he knew that he did not wish to be a minister. The choice of law, in fact, came easily to him, and though his practice at the bar was interrupted by some years of teaching at Cornell (an interruption in part dictated by the state of his health), his devotion to his profession was undoubted. When the call of public service came to him in 1905, he accepted the challenge, if not willingly, with a clear conviction of duty. At every stage of his career he gives the impression of a strength and self-confidence that win admiration and stamp him as a great personality.

Hughes had reason for this strength and self-confidence. He had superb intellectual equipment. At school he was always near the top of the class. At college he was graduated with high distinction. His memory was almost photographic, and his capacity for rapid reading phenomenal. In later life he could come very near to repeating verbatim a speech of substantial length which he had dictated to his stenographer; he could digest the materials presented to him with lightning speed. To these qualities he joined prodigious industry. Hughes worked at high tension and for long hours. Indeed, he often overworked and became nervous and irritable and needed (and took) substantial vacations. But in the main he carried a load that would have daunted a less able and vigorous man. In addition, contrary to a widespread assumption, Hughes was by no means lacking in the social gifts. He was never the solitary recluse, the "grind." He distinguished himself in college by joining a dinner club and a fraternity. His classmates regarded him as a leader and early recognized his ability as a speaker. When he graduated from Brown University, he had ample reason to believe in himself, as, fundamentally, he always did. There is no note of frustration or timidity in the story of his life.

But Hughes's assurance rested on more than confidence in his intellectual powers. The rigorous moral training that he received from his parents, though it did not lead him in all respects to accept their judgments, was highly important in his youthful development. His personal standards of conduct were of the highest; his notions of honor and right inflexible. Throughout his career he leaves the impression of a man convinced of his own rightness, not to the point of smugness or disagreeable complacency but to a degree striking in its impact. It is dangerous to believe in oneself too much; but it is also dangerous, and sometimes fatal in the large world of affairs, to believe in oneself too little. It cannot be said that Hughes suffered from this latter peril.

Despite self-confidence and ability Hughes did not enter public life at an early age. He was preoccupied with his profession and, from the beginning to the end of his life, he was primarily a lawyer. After college he taught school for a year to earn money to go to Columbia Law School, from which he was graduated with the highest honors in 1884. Three years later he joined the firm of Carter, Hughes and Cravath, which acted principally in the field of commercial paper litigation. Shortly thereafter, but only after he considered himself to be established, he married Antoinette Carter, the daughter of his senior partner. He was rigorous in the performance of his tasks as a lawyer, but the range of his cases was not particularly wide and in no way foreshadowed the sweep and ability which he was to show as a judge. He showed more evidence of his power when at the Cornell Law School in 1891 and 1892 he taught a broad range of subjects with much authority.

In 1893, Hughes returned to New York. With a growing family to support he stuck close to his last. No one would have suspected, even as late as 1904, that he had before him a brilliant political career.

What was Hughes's way of thought so far as politics was concerned? With what assumptions and what preconceptions did he enter public life? Once there, how did he view the problems of statesmanship? Was he a liberal or a conservative? Was he rigid or flexible in his mental outlook? These are questions we ought to try to answer at the outset.

It is not easy to find materials which bear upon Hughes's choice of the Republican Party as the party for him. He was the son of an abolitionist preacher; he came to young manhood at a period when there was precious little to attract one towards the Democrats (though perhaps something to repel one from their rivals); James A. Garfield was a member of his college fraternity, and Hughes seems to have taken it for granted that the Ohio statesman was the proper choice for the Presidency in 1880; and for some reason, though exposed to the low-tariff doctrines of the academics of the period at Brown, he does not seem to have been permanently affected by such teaching. Indeed, on the question of the tariff he continued during a large part of his active political life to indulge in the usual sophistries and illogic so long connected with that subject. All in all it is perhaps safe to say that the choice of the Republican Party as the party of his allegiance was natural enough for a youth of his background and of his associations, and that in the field of the law it was more natural still.

If one started with a slant towards the Grand Old Party, this slant was likely to be confirmed by the campaign of 1896. This campaign, waged by William Jennings Bryan on the free-silver issue, shook loose from their moorings many Democrats; and the evidence is ample that it consolidated the position of many who had before this year called themselves Republicans. In his distrust of the silver-tongued orator of the Democratic Party (its leading figure from 1896 to 1912) Hughes was typical of the economic and social group to which he belonged.

Party allegiance, however, frequently tells us very little about the thought of a given individual. A deeper question is the question as to whether Hughes is to be placed in the stream of conservative or liberal thought among the American political leaders. And this may well lead us to a brief digression as to what these words may be supposed to mean in connection with the political development of the United States. In the first place, there is no good reason for identifying the word conservative with reaction, or the word liberal with radicalism. The tendency in American politics has usually been towards the center; and few American statesmen have been the out-and-out apostles of retrogression, on the one hand, or of sweeping and dangerous measures of change, on the other, whatever the language of political invective. In this happy country of ours the middle course has usually been that of the mass of the electorate and of the vast majority of its leaders.

Yet there have been certain clear characteristics of the conservative point of view in the United States. Conservatives, for example, have frequently, perhaps usually, laid considerable stress on the checks and balances of the Constitution; and accordingly they have regarded with great respect the balancing role of the judiciary. Conservatives, also, have, on the whole, shown themselves more in sympathy with the actually operating American business system than their opponents and have valued more highly the entrepreneurial gifts which have done much to make our great industrial progress possible; and they have, perhaps, placed greater emphasis on sound and effective administration than those in the opposite camp. They have not necessarily been completely allergic to change; but they have been cautious in advocating it.

Judged in relation to these criteria, Hughes was a conservative. Certainly he believed, and believed deeply, in the role of the courts in our constitutional system; while he wished to see business purged of gross abuses, he was not critical of the American economic system itself; he had unusually strong administrative instincts; and in those periods of his life when he advocated reform, his proposals were cautious in their general tone. The slashing attack on the burden of armaments in his term as Secretary of State may be thought to be an exception; yet reduction of armaments, viewed from another angle of vision, was just such a policy as a sincere friend of the American business system would be most likely to propose. Many other of our political figures, such, for example, as Elihu Root, whose conservatism was beyond question, took the same view.

Yet in another sense Hughes fits into the liberal frame of reference. He was more sensitive to the necessity for change, less resistant to the forces making for change, than many conservatives. His humanitarianism (and humanitarianism is an essential part of American liberalism), while far removed from romanticism, while perhaps too intellectual and too little emotional, was often evidenced, especially in relation to the Negro. His devotion to the libertarian view of life in the field of ideas, to freedom of speech and of the press and of political association, was more characteristic of the liberal point of view than of its opposite. In his attitude toward social changes and toward the altering role of the United States in the world Hughes was more flexible, more disposed to accept the inevitability of adjustment, than many conservatives. All in all, therefore, it is unwise to categorize him in terms of a single adjective — liberal or conservative. His mind did not operate in terms of fixed theory; it was singularly practical.

But there is a point of view with regard to him which may provide us with the unifying factor in his long public career. This factor consists in the changing vistas of American life in the years of his maturity, in his adjustment to them, and in his part in the realization — or rejection — of new conceptions in the field of government and foreign policy.

Hughes grew up in an epoch of conservatism and laissez faire. There are few signs that he was much touched by the evils of that period until he entered public life in his middle forties. By then the American people were becoming more and more aroused to the fact that their business system was not perfect, and that some degree of governmental authority was needed to repress and correct its abuses. Hughes shared this sentiment. On the state level he was a leader in translating it into political terms. At the same time, on the national scene, Theodore Roosevelt was preaching the gospel of a more vigorous federal government and of a wider social consciousness. Here, also, Hughes responded. When he went to the Supreme Court bench in 1910, he was one of those judges who was sympathetic to the nationalistic tendency and to the processes of social reform.

Then came the First World War and the emergence of the United States on the stage of the world in a role more important than ever before. Hughes left the bench to participate actively in the controversies of that period as a candidate for the Presidency. When the struggle was over, he by no means accepted the dream of the future portrayed by Woodrow Wilson and, along with many other Americans — the majority, in fact — condemned any policy of entanglement. But as Secretary of State he was no little American, acting in a parochial spirit. He conducted the foreign affairs of the nation in a new frame of reference which took account of the changed position of the United States. At the same time he kept that connection with the past that is characteristic of his temperament and outlook. He was, in the realization of his objectives, one of the most successful of Secretaries and he broadened the scope of American diplomatic action.

It was the same when it came to his service as Chief Justice and his reaction to the reform measures of the New Deal. To some of the tendencies of the new era Hughes was far from friendly. He was bound to feel strongly when Roosevelt attacked the Court itself. But he never became, like four of his colleagues, an embittered opponent of what went on. Though he sometimes stood with the conservative judges in striking down New Deal legislation, in more than one key case he pronounced decisions which affirmed and consolidated the new order. On the whole he accepted it, seeking rather to guide than to nullify the changes. The Court in the years of his Chief Justiceship made wide adaptations to the new age. The Chief Justice participated in this process.

In the largest sense Hughes was a statesman. Statesmanship in a democratic community consists in the use of public authority to make the necessary adaptations to a changing political and social environment and to the demands of the time. Charles E. Hughes was one who understood this art.

Charles Evans Hughes *and* American Democratic Statesmanship

I
Hughes and New York Politics

HUGHES ENTERED PUBLIC LIFE at the age of forty-three. Up to that time, save for the teaching years at Cornell, he had occupied himself chiefly with the practice of his profession. He had been successful, but he could hardly have been described as widely known. His chief outside interest had been his Sunday-school class at the Fifth Avenue Baptist Church, best known as the church of John D. Rockefeller. He had not sought public service and had little interest in partisan political activity. Yet he was not without ambition, and he was the kind of man likely to respond to an appeal to perform a public duty.

The appeal came in 1905 when Senator Stevens, chairman of a joint legislative committee appointed to investigate the gas and electric industry in the City of New York, asked him to serve as counsel. Characteristically, Hughes satisfied himself as to the character and *bona fides* of the senator before accepting. Characteristically, too, he took up the assignment because he thought it would be cowardly to refuse. He had no especial experience in this particular field, but, as always, once he began to work, he quickly mastered the subject in hand. The investigation was conspicuous for the combination of suavity and force which he brought to his task. It resulted in a report in which the evils of the existing situation were pitilessly exposed without the slightest trace of demagogy. Hughes revealed that the City of New York was paying rates for electric service three times as high as those charged private consumers. He demonstrated that the gas trust itself was scandalously overcapitalized. He called attention to the shameful adulteration of gas at the risk of human life. And his report culminated in concrete recommendations for reductions in the price of both gas and electricity and, more important still, in a demand for the creation of an adequate regulatory commission "with inquisitorial authority, competent to make summary investigations of complaints, to supervise issues of securities and investment in the stocks or bonds of other companies, to regulate rates and to secure adequate inspection, or otherwise to enforce the provisions of the law."

Hughes's success at this job opened the door to a still-wider opportunity. Nineteen hundred five was the year of the great insurance scandals in New York City, first brought into public view as a result of a battle between James Hazen Hyde, the heir to a great fortune and to a controlling interest of the Equitable Life Insurance Company, and some of the other officers of the company. A joint committee of the legislature, constituted to conduct an investigation, asked Hughes to serve as counsel. He had just completed his previous task and was enjoying a well-deserved vacation in Europe. But once again, in obedience to the call of public duty, he accepted.

The hearings began in September of 1905 and lasted throughout the autumn. The gas investigation had been trivial in comparison. And what was of particular interest was the ruthless way in which the committee's counsel unveiled the connection between business and politics — and Republican politics at that. Hughes brought out the fact that the great insurance companies had contributed to campaign funds; he put on the stand such financial magnates as George W. Perkins and E. H. Harriman and compelled them to admit their part in the influencing of legislation at Albany; he exposed the almost arbitrary power exercised by the presidents of some of the greatest insurance concerns; and he dealt sharply, and yet courteously, with some of the best-known and most respected figures in the whole insurance field.

In the midst of his inquiry, in an attempt to divert him from his task, some of the Republican leaders in New York City proposed that he become the Republican candidate for mayor, but this offer was firmly refused. And, as in the case of the previous investigations, the inquiry itself was followed by a long list of recommendations for legislation, recommendations many of which were enacted in the legislative session of 1906 under the insistent spur of the investigator. The problems of the gas inquiry had been largely local; those in the insurance field were of virtually country-wide significance. Indeed, it is not too much to say that Hughes's work in this field was fundamental to the history of insurance regulation in general. To it he had brought the amazing grasp and industry which characterized him when he undertook the study of an important problem.

By this time the New York lawyer had become a national figure. The era was favorable to him. Reform was in the air. Distrust of concentrated wealth was widespread. In the White House, Theodore Roosevelt, triumphantly reinstalled in power after the election of 1904, was constantly inveighing against the forces of evil in business and demanding the acceptance of a higher standard of business morality. In addition, the Republican Party was in trouble in New York State. It was threatened by the rise of a powerful, if unscrupulous personality, who sought to capitalize the situation. William Randolph Hearst had entered the field of New York journalism in the 1890s. Steadily he had been building up his power, and the papers which he published were the facile instruments of his ambition. He had run for mayor of New York in 1905 and had come very near to being elected. Now he was on the verge of a cynical deal with the very Tammany Hall which he had challenged, with the governorship in view. There was every reason to believe that he would present a very real threat to Republican ascendancy and every necessity for nominating a strong man, and a liberal one, against him.

In Washington the situation was clearly understood. The President had evinced much interest in Hughes and had invited him to the White House in the spring of 1906. As the year lengthened and the specter of a Hearst victory became clearer, the administration, under the urging of some of the more farsighted Republican leaders, came to the point of actual intervention in the forthcoming campaign. At the Republican convention in September the President made it clear that he believed that Hughes was by far the strongest candidate that the convention could nominate. Though the bosses lamented this opinion, they were in no position to contest it, and when the time came for the choice to be made, Hughes was unanimously nominated. "I thank you for your confidence," he wired in reply. "I shall accept the nomination without pledge other than to do my duty according to my conscience. If elected, it will be my ambition to give the State a sane, efficient and honorable administration, free from taint of bossism or of servitude to any private interest."

The electoral conflict that followed was exceedingly bitter. The Republican candidate made a remarkably vigorous campaign, sometimes attending five or six rallies in an evening and making as many as twenty speeches in a single day. In some respects the most revealing incident of the canvass was an exchange of views between Hughes and Roosevelt. The President did not approve of a ticket for judicial office which had been selected by a committee of lawyers, of whom Hughes was one. He thought it did not contain sufficient recognition of the "organization" and, at the urging of the politicos, he made his views known to the campaigner. But he accomplished nothing whatsoever. For the first, but not for the last, time in his association with the Rough Rider, Hughes brushed aside the counsels of political expediency and rested his position upon the necessity for high competence in government. He was to give more evidence of his political austerity as time went on.

Notwithstanding this little episode the White House strongly backed the candidate, sending Elihu Root, perhaps the most distinguished member of the Cabinet, to speak for him, and making a personal statement in his behalf. And when election day came around, the results, on the whole, were satisfactory. It can hardly be said that Hughes won a resounding triumph. His plurality, in the neighborhood of 60,000, was due almost as much to the cutting of Hearst in New York City as it was to the majorities polled upstate for the Republican ticket. The New York editor proved to be a weak rather than a strong candidate. But the Democrats carried every office except the governorship, and it is probable that only a candidate with the positive virtues that Hughes possessed would have pulled through. There can be little question that, at the moment, the victor derived very great satisfaction indeed from the defeat of what he sincerely believed to be a demagogic campaign against the interests of the people.

Hughes made a very great contribution as governor of New York. There had been distinguished figures in the governor's mansion at Albany before 1907 and others were to follow. But far too often in the previous history of the state, the executive had been an amiable administrative chief carrying out his duties in routine fashion, often subject to the control of the political machine, and rarely asserting legislative leadership. In state as in national government our political system functions most effectively when there is a strong and dominating personality at the center of things, one who effectively represents a broad and general interest as against the congeries of special and local interests that beat upon any legislature. In his three years and ten months at Albany, Hughes set an example of effective action that was not only bracing to the people of New York State but also had an important influence outside. The techniques of Woodrow Wilson in New Jersey in 1911 and 1912 owed something, perhaps much, to the inspiration of this governor of New York.

Hughes's methods were not those of the conventional politician. He declined to use the weapon of patronage. Indeed, he went further. On one occasion, the national administration, acting on a suggestion from one of the governor's advisers, removed from office the collector of the port at Rochester, New York — one Archie Sanders, who had been hostile to the Hughes program. Much to the chagrin of President Roosevelt, Hughes issued a statement that he had not been consulted and knew nothing of the removal until it was announced to the public.

This extremely austere attitude towards the spoils of office was also revealed in other ways. At the outset of Hughes's first term the legislative leaders consulted the

Executive Mansion with regard to the chairmanship of committees. They were met with a flat rebuff. The governor did not intend to expose himself to demands for favors by intervening in what he considered to be the business of the legislators themselves.

This negative position with regard to the patronage was matched by a very positive point of view with regard to the rank and file of the voters. Fundamental to Hughes's tactics was the belief that if the voters could be brought to understand an issue, they would be willing to support him. Unlike his predecessors, Hughes met most of his visitors and transacted the public business in a large audience room to which anyone was welcome. The politicans and the people stood upon the same basis. The secret conference was no longer the principal engine of government. The deals that had characterized so many previous administrations were no part of his method. In addition the governor spent much time in making his views known. He cultivated the confidence of the newspapermen and often held two press conferences in the same day. He was an unwearied public speaker. On occasion, too, he intervened actively in local contests where he thought the integrity of his program was at stake. In a great battle over gambling legislation (to be considered later) he took a vigorous part in a special election and brought about a clean-cut victory for a much-needed supporter. He was never intimidated by opposition. He would speak as forthrightly to one type of audience as to another. He carried on a campaign of public education such as New York had never seen before.

Hughes had always a very deep interest in administration. Many reformers and many liberals are too deeply concerned with the process of legislation and too little concerned with the equally vital matter of seeing that legislation is made effective in practice. From the outset of his first term Hughes stood for competent conduct of the public business. One of the first challenges that he met in this regard had to do with the office of superintendent of elections in the metropolitan district. The candidate of the politicians, and the incumbent when the governor took office, was a Republican district leader in Brooklyn named Swasey, a mere tool of the machine. Both Timothy Woodruff, the chairman of the Republican State Committee, and Herbert Parsons, one of Hughes's most effective and honorable supporters in the city, urged his reappointment. Rebuffed in a long conversation with the governor that lasted until one in the morning, they appealed to the national administration in Washington and actually secured the intervention of the President himself. But Hughes stood his ground and, in a new affront to the chagrined Chief Executive, announced the choice of a successor to Swasey at the very moment of the meddling from the White House. Nor did Hughes consult the political leaders with regard to a superintendent of public works. He chose Senator Stevens of Attica, whom he had learned to trust in the gas investigation, and this despite the fact that Stevens was anathema to the powerful Wadsworth family, one of whose members was Speaker of the Assembly.

The governor demonstrated still more remarkable political independence in the matter of the superintendent of insurance. At the outset of the new administration this post was held by Otto Kelsey, an honorable man, with strong political backing from former Governor Odell and the Speaker. But Kelsey did not satisfy Hughes's standards of administrative efficiency. He seemed unable to do more than carry on the insurance department in a routine manner without much regard to the exposures and recommendations of the investigations of 1906. His professed willingness to do whatever he was directed to do hardly seemed to the governor the sign of a vigorous and imaginative administrator. Kelsey was strongly entrenched, however, and his removal required the assent of the Senate. In vain Hughes urged him to resign. The governor, resurrecting an old statute, summoned Kelsey to a hearing before recommending his dismissal, and in a public examination ruthlessly exposed the administrative failings of the superintendent. Still Kelsey hung on. The legislature delayed action for months and in May, by the close vote of 27 to 24, declined to acquiesce in Kelsey's removal. Hughes refused to accept defeat. He preferred charges against Kelsey and appointed a former assistant of his in the insurance investigation to look into the conduct of the department. Once again the Senate, this time by a vote of 30 to 19, refused to cooperate. Only after the re-election of the governor in 1908 did Kelsey finally relinquish his office.

Hughes was of course occasionally at fault in his choice of public servants. After a long search, in 1907, in the midst of a critical situation, the governor appointed Luther Mott, the son of a Republican state committeeman, head of the Banking Department. But when after a brief period Mott demonstrated his inability to grapple with a difficult problem, Hughes compelled him to resign and managed to get a banker of wide reputation to take over the post. Undoubtedly in this instance he acted late and, it may be, without complete understanding of the seriousness of the whole matter. His enemies were prompt to attribute to him some of the responsibility for the banking crisis itself. But in the long run Hughes learned from his error and came forward with some constructive proposals for banking reform.

A too-little-noticed reform of the Hughes period in the administrative field was the Moreland Act, a source of immense strength to future governors. This act authorized and directed the governor to carry on executive investigations not only in the state field but with regard to city and county officials as well. Under it the governor brought charges of gross negligence against the presidents of the boroughs of Manhattan, the Bronx, and Queens, and removed them from office. He wielded the new weapon placed in his hands with courage and effect.

But Hughes was not only an effective administrator. He was also the leader in the enactment of a legislative program. In the four years of his governorship he was responsible for a very substantial amount of progressive legislation and for the recommendation of other measures which time has approved. Indeed, this was the period in his life most closely identified with the progressive point of view. As we have said, the spirit of the time was favorable to reform; the example of the national administration and the prodigious popularity of the President pointed the way towards progressive legislation; and the necessity for rooting out business abuses had been underlined for Hughes himself by the gas and insurance investigations. In addition there was always the reasonable contention that the correction of abuse was not only sound liberalism but sound conservatism. Hughes, like the man in the White House, was the friend of moderate change in no small measure because he hated excess and feared demagoguery and radicalism.

By far the most important legislative measure of the two Hughes administrations was the enactment of the bill for the creation of two public-service commissions, one for the City of New York and one for upstate. It is difficult for us at this day to realize how novel was the type of regulation proposed by the governor. In the national field the Interstate Commerce Commission Act, as revised in 1906, went part of the way along the same path; but this measure proved inadequate and had to be revised in 1910. In the state field nothing much had yet been done to establish regulatory commissions with rate-fixing powers, although Wisconsin was to enact a law in the same year as New York.

The New York law was not only a pioneering statute; it was also drawn with regard to certain fixed principles that gave it a cardinal importance. The basic conception was simple. The commissions it created were to have the power to act upon their own initiative as well as upon complaint; they were to pass upon the issue of stocks and bonds (something not prescribed for the railroads in national legislation until 1921); they were to examine properties, books, and accounts; to fix reasonable rates; to require adequate and impartial service; to provide for the safety of employees and for the protection of the public; and generally to direct whatever might be necessary and proper to safeguard the public interest and to secure the fulfillment of the public obligations of the corporations under their supervision. They could act, of course, only after providing for a thorough hearing and investigation.

Hughes was responsible for two provisions in this legislation that have been fundamental to the development of administrative tribunals in this country. In the first place he insisted that the commissions should operate without interference by the courts unless they exceeded their statutory authority or violated the constitution of the state or of the United States. The favorite expedient of corporations in resisting administrative control in this period was an appeal to the judiciary. The Interstate Commerce Commission, originally created in 1887, had long been hamstrung by the constant recourse of the railroads to this expedient. Administrative action could be rendered almost nugatory if every decision of the administrative body was to be brought before the judges and, at the same time, as the governor pointed out, a burden could be thrown upon the courts too great for them to bear. Indeed, the whole principle of administrative action could by this means be nullified in practice. It is not strange that in the battle over this legislation the question of appeal bulked larger than any other issue, and that the Hughes position was sharply challenged by the representatives of the business interests.

Hughes fought tenaciously for his point of view. He fought the more readily because he was convinced, as a lawyer and as a believer in the American judicial system, that nothing could be more detrimental to the courts than to overburden them with the details of the regulatory power. Where a constitutional issue was involved he pointed out, in perhaps the most effective of his speeches on the issue, that no one could divest the courts of their authority. But beyond this it was unwise to go. "I have the highest regard for the courts," he said at Elmira on May 3, 1907. "My whole life has been spent in work conditioned upon respect for the courts. I reckon him one of the worst enemies of the community who will talk lightly of the dignity of the bench. We are under a Constitution, but the Constitution is what the judges say it is, and the judiciary is the safeguard of our liberty and of our property under the Constitution. I do not want to see any direct assault upon the courts, nor do I want to see any indirect assault upon the courts. And I tell you, ladies and gentlemen, no more insidious assault could be made upon the independence and esteem of the judiciary than to burden it with these questions of administration — questions which lie close to the public impatience, and in regard to which the people are going to insist on having administration by officers directly accountable to them." And in the same speech he declared, "With the courts giving a series of decisions in these administrative matters hostile to what the public believes, and free from that direct accounting to which administrative officers are subject, you will soon find a propaganda advocating a short-term judiciary, and you will turn upon our courts — the final safeguard of our liberties — that hostile and perhaps violent criticism from which they should be shielded and will be shielded if left with the jurisdictions which it was intended they should exercise."

It is worth pausing for a moment to consider the significance of the lines that have just been quoted. They indicate something fundamental; they indicate the governor's view that the security of the courts depends upon the way in which they exercise their power. They are far removed from that kind of mysticism which sees in action of the judiciary something sacrosanct and above the level of public criticism. They are the views of a statesman, not of a legal pedant or mere conformist.

The second principle on which Hughes insisted was the principle of centralized responsibility. And here again his view was a broad one, cutting to the root of a principle of sound administration, far removed from a mere yearning for personal power. The vice of the American governmental system — or at any rate one of its vices — lies in the diffusion of power and in the official irresponsibility which often goes with the diffusion of power. In this specific instance the foes of the governor demanded that the removal of the members of the Public Service Commission be brought about only with the consent of the Senate. The demand was intrinsically and fundamentally unsound. Hughes argued effectively against it in the Elmira speech already quoted. "No removability except by the Senate means incompetent and inefficient administration, and in the long run political administration. I do not care who is Governor, in the long run the one safeguard of the American people is responsible government with power adequate to meet the responsibility and accountability to the people for the exercise of that power. . . . In your Mayor and in your Governor, and in others entrusted with administrative powers, you must repose confidence. And if these men really stand, not in some secluded nook, protected by some statute passed without due regard to the public interest, but directly before the bar of public opinion, in the long run the people will get their due."

In both the essential points which he had raised with regard to public-service regulation Hughes was successful in securing the adoption of his point of view. The legislation enacted in 1907 conformed in almost every respect to his desires. He had built up such a body of opinion as made it impossible for a hostile legislature to resist him. In a few months of office he had won a great legislative victory and he had done it by methods which were as austere as they were effective.

If the passage of the Public Service Commission Act was probably the most fundamental of the laws of the Hughes period, the most dramatic battle took place in 1908 in the struggle over the question of race-track gambling. The New York constitution of 1894, as amended in 1905, contained an absolute prohibition against "any lottery, the sale of lottery tickets, pool-selling, book-making or any other kind of gambling." But, in carrying out this constitutional mandate, the legislature had passed an ambiguous statute which provided that if no tokens of race-track wagers were delivered, the only penalty for such gambling would be a civil suit for recovery of losses. In other words, it had set at naught the constitution itself.

The governor's message of 1908 called attention to this situation. But Hughes, in this matter, did not take the sole, or even the chief, initiative. There was a strong public sentiment, particularly in upstate New York, against this evasion of the fundamental law. The introduction of a repeal measure, the Agnew-Hart bill, does not appear to have been instigated by the governor.

Writing in 1954, one is aware of a change in the climate of opinion with regard to race-track gambling that makes it a little difficult to recapture the emotions of forty-six years ago. But to Hughes the issue was not the issue of gambling itself. He had no narrow attitude on this matter.

What concerned him was the violation of the constitution. Respect for legality was at the bottom of his increasingly strong and determined support of the bill. True, as the struggle proceeded, there is evident in some of his speeches a pretty strong conviction as to the evils that accompany this particular pastime. But the fundamental issue lay deeper and it came to engage his deepest emotions.

The battle that he waged on this matter was one of the bitterest of his career, and it brought down on his head the sincere loathing of many of the machine politicians of his own party. In the legislative session of 1908 the Agnew-Hart bill passed the Assembly by a highly satisfactory majority. But in the Senate, after a hot fight, it was defeated by a tie vote of 25 to 25. But the governor refused to be dismayed. The legislature adjourned on April 23. He called it back in special session for May 11. And, at the same time (and this no doubt reinforced his decision to resummon the legislators), he took advantage of the death of one of the senators in the Niagara-Orleans district to order a special election in that district.

In some of his earlier speeches Hughes had disavowed all intention of interfering with the prerogatives of the legislators and he had, as we have seen, taken a very austere view with regard to the patronage. But he now plunged into the fight in the Niagara-Orleans district with all his energy. "Rise in your might," he urged the voters. And though the voters did not obey this injunction on quite the scale which he might have wished, a supporter of repeal was sent back to Albany.

The closing scenes of the legislative battle were as dramatic as any ever seen at the state capital. The decisive vote rested with Senator Foelker of Brooklyn, who had, not long before, undergone an operation for appendicitis and who was by no means recovered when the time for voting came. But Hughes had the railroad train stop at Staatsburg to put the senator on board, and Foelker, despite maneuvers to prolong the debate and so to drive him from the Chamber, was able to cast the decisive vote. Through sheer tenacity, and once again through his direct appeal to public opinion, the governor had won a great victory.

In the third of his major legislative battles Hughes was less successful. The Republican Party in New York had for years been boss-ridden. Hughes had had ample demonstration of this fact. It is not strange, therefore, that he came to favor one of those party expedients which were popular at the time, one which offered some hope of enlarging the role of the ordinary voter in the management of party affairs. This was the direct primary. But on this question Hughes took a point of view very far from radical. He *did* originally recommend a system of direct nominations for all elective officers except presidential electors. But reflection modified his views. He digested, and apparently was influenced by, the arguments directed against this much-discussed reform. He saw the opportunity presented to the demagogue by the primary and he understood the dangers to coherent party organization. His ideal was responsible party government, not some system of riotous political individualism. Accordingly he modified his original proposal and suggested instead of state-wide primaries a kind of federal system. By this system the state was to be divided into primary districts, in each of which a committeeman was to be elected. The committeemen in each Assembly district would meet to select their candidate for the Assembly. Larger groups of the same committeemen would meet to select the candidates for the state Senate in the Senate districts. The Assembly committees would each select one delegate to a state-wide meeting which would select the state-wide candidates and draw up a state platform.

It is difficult to believe that this very modest scheme of reform would have done much to loosen the grip of the professional politicians. But with their usual myopia the Republican leaders rejected it out of hand. Men like Barnes, the arbitrary boss of the Albany machine, Woodruff, the sinuous chairman of the Republican State Committee, and James Wadsworth, the extremely conservative Speaker of the Assembly, would have nothing to do with this plan. Despite the fact that Hughes was backed by Elihu Root, just elected to the United States Senate, and despite his public appeals, the primaries bill was defeated in the New York upper house in 1909 by a vote of 112 to 28. In the session of 1910, Hughes returned to the attack. At Albany, while the legislature was still in session, he launched a terrific assault upon the bosses. But once again the Assembly defeated the proposed reform.

The governor was not yet finished. In June of 1910, Theodore Roosevelt returned from Africa and Europe. Hughes met him at the Harvard commencement. Pleading with him once more to enter the political arena in behalf of progressive government and appealing to him on the ground that silence would mean opposition, Hughes persuaded the former President to take up the cudgels in behalf of primary legislation. He had already called the legislature back in special session and this time he hoped, with Roosevelt's prestige to help him, that he might win success. Once again, however, the politicians at Albany were able to defy him. Once again the Assembly, ignoring the Hughes plan, responded with hostility, passing a purely "fake" primaries bill. The defeat was final.

The struggle over primary legislation was symptomatic of the declining influence which Hughes exercised in his second term. Though he had been re-elected in 1908 by a somewhat larger plurality than in 1906, he had not been able substantially to alter the character of the Republican organization, or to loosen the grip of the machine leaders. By his appeals to the people and by his tenacity and courage he had indeed only further embittered them. He found his job increasingly exacting and difficult. It is no wonder that he accepted the nomination to the Supreme Court when the opportunity came.

Furthermore, the primary fight marks an interesting moment in the association of Hughes with Theodore Roosevelt. The relations between the two men were by no means uniformly happy. Hughes, as we have seen, had irritated Roosevelt profoundly by his attitude towards party patronage and by his determination to pursue an independent course free of White House influence. When Hughes began to be talked of for President in 1908, the Rough Rider took a distinctly unfriendly position to his candidacy. When in January of that year the governor was about to make an important speech outlining his views with regard to national affairs, Roosevelt deliberately blanketed it with a sensational message from the White House. He virtually imposed upon the Republican convention the choice of Taft as his successor. And writing to the Republican candidate in the summer of 1908, he said, "Hughes is not a man I care for." But this critical view was modified soon thereafter. Hughes's first important campaign utterance outside New York, the Youngstown speech of October, immensely pleased the President. So, too, did the speeches in the West that followed. By the end of the campaign the two men were on cordial terms again, and this cordiality was still existent in 1910. There could hardly have been two people more different in temperament than Theodore Roosevelt and Charles E. Hughes, the one ebullient, indiscreet, violent and opportunist in politics, the other instinctively fair-minded even when pressing a cause, the soul of prudence and of political austerity. That these two men could cooperate effectively at all is a commentary on the strength of party loyalty in the United States.

Finally, with regard to the primary fight, it is to be observed that it was Hughes who first brought the former President back into politics. We need not attach too much importance to this fact. Roosevelt was congenitally incapable of inaction. If it had not been Hughes, it would have been someone else. Yet, considering the significance of T.R.'s re-entry on the political stage, it is worth noting that the appeal for that re-entry came from the quarter that it did.

Hughes's record as governor was rich in other legislation. Perhaps the most important in principle, though not in immediate effect, was a workmen's compensation act. This statute was a moderate one, making provision for compensation compulsory only in especially hazardous industries, and even so it was declared unconstitutional by the New York Court of Appeals. But it was in point of time one of the earliest enactments on this subject and it called attention to a serious problem. Indeed, it set the example for a spate of legislation on this problem which enforced the principle of compensation in virtually every important industrial state in the Union.

Although his administration saw the enactment of numerous other laws for the benefit of labor, Hughes made a more important contribution to the advancement of the conservation movement in New York State. Here again what seems commonplace today was by no means commonplace in the first decade of the century. The lavish granting away of public property for private use had only just begun to arouse the public conscience. President Roosevelt had dramatized the issue. The governor followed in part in his footsteps.

But in some respects Hughes went further. He appointed a commission to deal with the subject of water power. On the basis of its report Hughes recommended that only the state should build and own regulatory or power-generating reservoirs on streams originating or flowing through public parks or reservations and that hydroelectric projects might, even more widely, be undertaken by the state when such action appeared feasible and in the public interest. Such recommendations, in the year 1910, were about as far to the left as any public man in a position of leadership was likely to go.

On one important question Hughes took the conservative point of view. In 1910, Congress had submitted to the states a constitutional amendment authorizing the federal government to levy an income tax, "from whatever source derived." The governor opposed this amendment, asserting that its language would make possible the taxation of income derived from state and municipal securities and would thus increase the cost of borrowing for state and local agencies. He perhaps overstated the matter when in a message to the legislature he declared that if the income tax proposal were adopted, it would make the performance of local government a matter of national grace. But his point of view was accepted by the legislature, and afterwards, when the amendment was ratified, the courts so construed it as virtually to accept Hughes's point of view.

In the same way the governor stood on the conservative side in the veto of a two-cent-fare bill in the legislative session of 1908. Characteristically, he refused to sign this legislation because it had been enacted without investigation and without full determination of the facts. Not caprice but equitable administrative judgment was what he stood for in the regulation of public utilities.

In general Hughes's governorship is one of the most remarkable and perhaps one of the too-little-noticed parts of his career. It must be conceded that he accomplished no long-term reform in the structure of the Republican Party in New York State and indeed his very virtues made him incapable of effective organization politics. But this criticism ought not to obscure his very great services and achievements. His two terms of office revealed him as sensitive to the demands of the time, as open to new ideas, as sympathetic with social progress and with social reform. They revealed him (and I desire to repeat the point) as one of those liberals who saw clearly the importance of sound administration to the cause of liberalism. They revealed him also as a political leader of great force, with a strong faith in the people, and with a remarkable capacity for speaking to them. In much of Hughes's career, and necessarily so in his service on the bench, the note of moral passion, so characteristic of the man, is necessarily less frequently sounded. In the period of the governorship, it is constant and insistent.

But we may, perhaps, go further than this. The office of state governor had in many instances, at the turn of the century, become hardly more than ornamental, so much so that James Bryce, in *The American Commonwealth,* had written that the men who managed state governments turned out to be insignificant persons who failed to stir the public interest. Hughes demonstrated what a strong man in the governor's chair could do. Like Robert La Follette of Wisconsin, a very different type of person, he rehabilitated the office itself. And in rehabilitating the office he quickened and fortified the interest of the people in state government. It is on that quickened interest that the success, in some measure, of our federal system depends.

II

Associate Justice of the Supreme Court

THE RECORD MADE BY HUGHES as governor of New York brought him to the attention of the nation. That he should be thought of for national service was in no way surprising, and his nomination to the Supreme Court of the United States in 1910 by President Taft met with almost universal favor. The Court itself was hardly at its apogee at the time. Four of its judges were over seventy; the Chief Justice, Melville W. Fuller, was far past his peak; and a fifth justice was ill. In view of what was to follow many years later, it is interesting to observe that Taft himself alluded to the reluctance of those "old fools" to retire, and was irked at the way in which the four men on the bench who were over seventy threw "the work and the responsibility on the other five." Hughes himself was only forty-eight; he could scarcely fail to have a tonic influence; and the President even went so far as to hold before him the lure of the Chief Justiceship in case of the death or resignation of Fuller. It was natural enough that the New York governor should accept the challenge.

Thus began almost six years of judicial service, six years during which Hughes markedly influenced American constitutional law and national and social progress.

Before embarking upon a study of this period, it is highly important for the reader to understand, with more exactness than is often the case, the precise role of the Supreme Court of the United States.

It is a well-known fact that the Court exercises the right to declare of no effect both national and state enactments which conflict with the Constitution of the United States or with treaties made under its authority. This right, so far as a state statute is concerned, was asserted as early as 1796 (*Ware v. Hylton*). In the case of a federal law it was first assumed, in the case of *Marbury v. Madison,* in the year 1803. Sparingly used in the period prior to the Civil War, it became a more and more significant feature of the work of the Court in the years that followed. Today it is beyond dispute a well-established feature of American jurisprudence; nor can there be the slightest question that the great majority of the American people believe in the principle of judicial review.

But opinions have differed, and do differ, as to what the practice implies. One extreme, the rigidly legalistic view, assumes that the construction of the Constitution is a matter from which all emotional prepossessions can and ought to be excluded. The language of the Constitution, those who hold this view maintain, is clear. The duty of the judges is merely to apply that language to the case in hand. If assistance is needed, the numerous precedents created in a hundred and fifty years will be available, and those precedents should be followed in accordance with the judicial doctrine of *stare decisis.*

At the other pole of thought is the view that constitutional construction is a matter of judicial caprice. Those who take this position (and this again is an extreme position) call attention to the very general language of the Constitution. What, for example, is meant by the general grant to Congress of the power to "regulate commerce among the states and with the Indian tribes"? John Marshall was able to deduce from these words the power to create a national bank. Was he not reading into the fundamental document his own strong Federalist predilection with regard to the extension of national power? Or what is meant by the provision of the Fourteenth Amendment that the states shall deprive no person of "life, liberty, or property without due process of law"? In 1905 five judges read into this clause the conclusion that a New York statute limiting the hours of work in bakeshops to ten hours a day was a deprivation of the liberty of the workers; were not these judges influenced by their social prejudices? Such is the argument brought forward by those who criticize the Court, and in its extreme form it suggests that constitutional decisions are hardly matters of law at all, in the strict sense of the term.

Now the truth lies between the two extremes. Judges,

in the nature of their calling, are disposed to approach a problem intellectually, not in an emotional dither (though exceptions occur). They are in the habit of paying respect to precedent. They prefer to nibble away at previous decisions they regard as antiquated, rather than flatly to abandon *stare decisis*. Against their human desire to see the law correspond with what the law perhaps ought to be is their natural instinct to respect the law as it is. On the other hand, there is undeniable merit in the contention that the broad language of the Constitution and even the precedents themselves frequently permit choices to be made. As a very penetrating student of the Hughes Court has pointed out, this fact "permits inarticulate and unavowed considerations, conscious or unconscious, to play an important part in determinations of constitutionality." The fact must be clearly understood by anyone who attempts, in a truly objective spirit, to analyze the Court's decisions.

Surely Charles Evans Hughes understood this. In the Elmira speech of 1907, from which we have already quoted, he had declared, "We are under a Constitution, but the Constitution is what the judges say it is." He was later to resent the use of this phrase by the critics of the Court in the constitutional struggle of 1937. But a year later, he said almost the same thing again. "Congress may pass laws, but the Supreme Court interprets and construes them, and determines their validity. The Constitution, with its guarantees of liberty, and its grants of Federal power, is finally what the Supreme Court determines it to mean." In the same year, in supporting the candidacy of William Howard Taft for the Presidency, he frankly appealed for the Republican candidate on the ground that he would probably have in his hands the appointment of four of the Supreme Court judges. "Upon the learning, wisdom and character of the judges of the Supreme Court rests not merely the just determination of the important matters of private right which come before that august tribunal, but to a very large degree the course of our political history and the development and security of our institutions."

Hughes did not come, then, to the bench with any limited view of the power he might there exercise. He recognized the portentous authority that under the Constitution was placed in his hands. In his first term of service he substantially affected the development of American constitutional law in terms of the extension of national power, of the just role of the rights of the individual as against the state, of the reconciliation of liberty with authority. It is not possible with complete accuracy to measure his role. The Court decides cases in private conference. It is a first principle of judicial propriety not to reveal what goes on there. In many matters not on the surface this relatively young and vigorous man may conceivably have exercised an important influence. But there is evidence enough from those instances in which he spoke for the Court, or in which he exercised the right of dissent, to assign him an important role in our jurisprudence.

In the years of Hughes's service there did not exist that deep division in the Court which was to manifest itself in the years of his Chief Justiceship. Differences of opinion there were; but it is not possible to think of the new judge as having determined the trend of judicial thinking. He was representative of a broad tendency within the body of the Court itself. And yet the many cases in which he spoke for the Court attest both his intellectual powers and his capacity for leadership.

Those powers were severely tested by issues raised in the heated climate of opinion of the years 1910 to 1916. These were the years when the Progressive movement burgeoned in American politics; they were the years of Theodore Roosevelt's New Nationalism. The social conscience of America was deeply stirred, and the reforms then proposed called for fresh thinking as to the limits of national and state power, as to the relationship of government to the disadvantaged, and as to the nature of law itself. It is amongst Hughes's claims to greatness that while he never trimmed his sails to the popular breeze, in any mean sense of the term, he understood and sought to interpret the larger demands of the time. In this spirit he faced his first tour of duty in Washington.

In the development of the American constitutional system one of the most important questions is that of centralization versus decentralization. What powers are to be conceded to the national government? What powers are to be reserved to the states? No American wishes to see a kind of gigantism develop in Washington. Yet with the increasing complexity of national life, the number of problems national in scope and calling for national action is greater. In seeking a just balance between state power and federal power, the Supreme Court of the United States must play a central role.

The most important aspect of this problem in the second decade of the century was in the regulation of interstate commerce, and specifically in railroad legislation. We must remember that the whole idea of such regulation was not very old in 1910. Congress had enacted the Interstate Commerce Commission Act in 1887, but this statute had been largely ineffective in securing the ends to which it was directed until after the supplemental legislation of 1906 and 1910. The question of its practical scope came before the Court in the years following, and in two cases of fundamental import, the Minnesota rate cases and the Shreveport case, it was Hughes who delivered the opinion of the Court, speaking in the first instance for a unanimous bench, and in the second case for seven of its nine members. In these two important cases, Hughes assumed a progressive attitude in the sense that he accepted and foresaw that wider role for the government at Washington that experience has proved necessary.

In the Minnesota cases he performed a service of the first order and a duty rarely assigned to a newly seated justice. The problem of the limits of federal regulation of the railroads was extremely complicated. In judicial conference, indeed, so many angles of the problem were brought up that some of the judges were doubtful whether an opinion could be written that would deal adequately with the subject. But Chief Justice White gave the problem to Hughes, who responded in a monumental decision, involving months of work and covering over one hundred pages in the Supreme Court reports. Hughes was by no means unmindful of the rights of the states in his opinion; indeed, the Minnesota rate cases affirmed state authority. But they did much more. They opened the door to the extension of federal authority as well.

On the heels of these decisions came the Shreveport case. It was shown in this case that certain rail rates entirely within the state of Texas discriminated against rates set between certain points in Texas and Shreveport, Louisiana. The Court sustained the Interstate Commerce Commission in setting aside these *intra*state rates.

The far-reaching consequences of these decisions "can hardly be exaggerated," in the judgment of one of the best balanced commentators on Hughes's judicial career. They recognized a "federal authority adequate to the molding of an integrated system of transportation without regard to state boundaries which had little practical reality in the actual conduct of the commerce of the nation." These decisions, Professor Hendel observes, "contributed greatly to fostering a recognition by the Court that the conflict between national and state power, with regard to the regulation of the commerce of the nation, could be resolved only in terms of practical effect." And finally, "if it be recognized that intrastate transportation rates may, for practical reasons, be controlled by federal authority so far as they vitally affect interstate commerce, does it not follow that intrastate *production* may for similar reasons be constitutionally controlled by the federal government in so far as it may vitually affect interstate commerce?" This question was to prove of the greatest importance later when Hughes became Chief Justice, and when the Wagner Labor Relations Act was before the Court.

The rate cases are by no means the only ones in which Hughes indicated that he took the broad view of the commerce clause. In an important decision he sustained congressional legislation regulating the hours of labor of railroad employees in interstate commerce. In another he took a broad view of the employers' liability acts of 1906 and 1908, holding that they barred retroactively contracts intended to exempt the railroad corporations from payments for damages. Yet he was never the blind advocate of centralization. "An over-centralized government," he declared in a speech before the American Bar Association, "would break down of its own weight. . . . If there were centered in Washington a single source of authority from which proceeded all the governmental forces of the country — created and subject to its will — upon whose permission all legislative and administrative action depended throughout the length and breadth of this broad land, I think we should swiftly demand and set up a different system. If we did not have states, we should speedily have to create them." His way of thinking on the problem of federal and state sovereignty was never doctrinaire. It was grounded in the solid realities of the national life, as he conceived and interpreted them.

Hughes also sided with the forces of the future when he dealt with the limits of state power. These issues were raised by the construction of the Fifth and the Fourteenth Amendments, which provide, the one for the federal government, the other for the states, that "no person shall be deprived of life, liberty, or property, without due process of law." The precise meaning of this phrase "due process of law" has again and again caused divisions in the Court. A narrow construction would suggest that it was designed to protect the citizen against the violation of those *procedures* deemed essential to the protection of his rights. But the Courts have taken a wider view, and have again and again insisted on reading *substantive* restrictions into the language just quoted. In others words, they have insisted that legislation must meet some standard of reasonableness which they themselves set up. Obviously, there is room here for wide difference of opinion, and for what the censorious would be apt to describe as an abuse of judicial power.

The argument against invoking the Fourteenth Amendment to void social legislation in the states was stated in classical form by Justice Holmes five years before Hughes appeared upon the Court. In 1905 there came before the Tribunal a New York statute limiting the hours of work in bakeshops to ten hours a day. By a five-to-four vote it was declared unconstitutional, and Holmes was one of the dissenters. "This case is decided," he wrote, "upon an economic theory which a large part of the country does not entertain. If it were a question whether I agreed with the theory, I should desire to study it further and long before making up my mind. But I do not conceive that to be my duty because I strongly believe that agreement or disagreement has nothing to do with the right of a majority to embody their opinions in law. It is settled by various decisions of this Court that state constitutions and state laws may regulate life in many ways which we as legislators might think as injudicious or, if you like, as tyrannical as this, and which equally with this interfere with the liberty to contract. . . . The Fourteenth Amendment does not enact Mr. Herbert Spencer's 'Social Statics' . . . A constitution is not intended to embody a particular economic theory, whether of paternalism and the organic relation of the citizen to the state or of laissez faire. It is made for people of fundamentally differing views, and the accident of our finding certain opinions natural and familiar or novel and shocking ought not to conclude our judgment upon the question whether statutes embodying them conflict with the Constitution of the United States."

Holmes's earlier protest, though rendered in a dissenting opinion, influenced the Court substantially in the period of Hughes's service. In some very interesting key cases, state legislation which might have fallen under the ban was sustained, and sustained by a unanimous vote. Many of these cases dealt with the position of the worker. In several of them Hughes spoke for all the nine justices, and the fact that he wrote the decisions is significant. Thus, he delivered the opinion in a case in which the Court upheld an Iowa statute barring a railroad corporation from setting up as a defense, in an action of negligence for injury suffered by an employee, a prior contract of indemnity or insurance. In another, he affirmed the validity of a statute prohibiting the employment of children under sixteen years of age in various hazardous occupations, and barring the defense that the employer acted in good faith. In still a third, he declined to set aside a California law forbidding the employment of women in selected establishments for more than eight hours a day.

In the most important labor case in which the Court divided (*Coppage v. Kansas*), Hughes was one of the dissenting justices. This case involved the constitutionality of a statute which made it a criminal offense for an employer to require as a condition of employment that an employee enter into an agreement not to join a union. The court split six to three. In associating himself with Mr. Justice Day in refusing to void the statute, Hughes again showed not only a sympathetic view of the position of the worker but his reluctance to stretch the Fourteenth Amendment. At the same time, and this was characteristic, he declined to go as far as he might have gone. Some years before in the Adair case the Court had invalidated a statute which made it a crime for an interstate carrier to discharge an employee because of membership in a labor union. Logically, if the reasoning in the Coppage case was sound, the Adair case should have been overruled. But the Justice, in associating himself with Day's dissent, attempted to maintain that the two cases were entirely different, and were controlled by different principles. It is not easy to see the validity of this reasoning. Here, as in a few other instances, Hughes's thought has an element of the metaphysical; the hypercritical would say of the sophistical. But a more charitable judgment would be that his deep concern for the continuity and the consistency of the law has in it something admirable, whatever the judgment of this specific matter.

Hughes's generally favorable attitude toward labor in construing the Fourteenth Amendment extended to the disadvantaged in a series of other decisions. One of the first in which he spoke for the Court involved the validity of an Alabama "peonage" statute. The law in question provided that any person who entered into a written contract of service, and who borrowed from his employer on the basis of this service, with intent to defraud from the outset, and then defaulted was guilty of a crime and punishable as in the case of theft. An amendment to this statute made failure to perform the service *prima facie* evidence of such intent, and did not permit the employee defendant to testify that he had not so intended. This legislation was challenged under the Thirteenth Amendment abolishing slavery and under a congressional statute passed in implementation of the amendment which declared null and void any state law which maintained or established "the voluntary or involuntary service or labor of any persons as peons in liquidation of any debt or obligation." Hughes, speaking for seven of the judges, declared the Alabama law unconstitutional. "Compulsory payment of service for a debt," he declared, "is peonage. We cannot escape the conclusion that although the statute, by its terms, is to punish fraud, still its natural and inevitable effect is to expose to conviction for crime those who simply fail or refuse to perform contracts for personal service in liquidation of a debt, and judging its purpose by its effect that it seeks in this way to provide the means of compulsion through which the performance of such service may be secured."

Even when Hughes failed effectively to aid the colored man, he nevertheless was able to assert a principle later to find more complete sanction. The state of Oklahoma had enacted a law authorizing intrastate carriers to provide sleeping cars, dining cars, and chair cars for white persons only. Hughes, and four other justices, believed this statute violated the constitutional injunction against state legislation denying the equal protection of the laws. But those who started suit under this legislation had proceeded carelessly, and counsel for the Negroes who appeared as plaintiffs was unable to show that any Negro had applied for, and been denied, accommodation. In the absence of a specific subject of complaint it was therefore impossible to set aside the law. But Hughes made his position perfectly clear. In his opinion he dismissed, as without merit, the contention that the lack of demand for first-class accommodations on the part of Negroes justified the statute. "It makes the constitutional right depend," he wrote, "upon the number of persons who may be discriminated against whereas the essence of the constitutional right is that it is a personal one." Thus, he at least paved the way for future decisions which made such discrimination impossible.

In an interesting case regarding aliens, Hughes delivered the opinion of the Court. An Arizona statute had required employers of more than five workers within the state to employ not less than eighty per cent qualified electors or native-born citizens of the United States. The statute was set aside by a unanimous vote under that clause of the Constitution and of the Fourteenth Amendment which declares that no state shall "deny to any person within its jurisdiction the equal protection of the laws." Certain regulations with regard to aliens, the Justice ruled, might be admissible. "But this does not make it possible," he went on, "to deny to lawful inhabitants because of their race or nationality, the ordinary means of earning a livelihood. It requires no argument to show that the right to work for a living in the common occupations of the community is of the very essence of the personal freedom and opportunity that it was the purpose of the Amendment to secure."

Finally, Hughes played an important part in the Frank case, celebrated for its connection with a ferocious explosion of anti-Semitic sentiment in Georgia. Frank, a young manager of a pencil factory in Atlanta, was accused of murdering a girl who worked for him. He had been tried under circumstances which strongly suggested the intimidation of the jury. The trial was conducted in a heated atmosphere and was interrupted at least once by applause from the spectators. The jury was polled at a time when there was an uproarious crowd outside the courtroom which was clearly attempting to influence the verdict. So great was the danger of violence that the accused had been advised by his counsel to remain out of the room while the jury rendered its decision.

The Supreme Court of the State of Georgia had twice reviewed the events surrounding the trial but had failed to discover any circumstances justifying a new one. Frank's lawyers had then sued for a writ of habeas corpus in the federal district court on the ground of the Fourteenth Amendment, and the case came to the Supreme Court on appeal. The majority of the Court denied the writ, in a long and highly technical opinion rendered by Mr. Justice Pitney. But Hughes and Holmes dissented. The opinion bears the name of the latter, but Hughes played an active part in drafting it. We may take it, therefore, that he wholly agreed with the statement that this was not a "matter for polite presumptions; we must look facts in the face. We think the presumption overwhelming that the jury responded to the passions of the mob. It is our duty to act upon the facts and to declare lynch law as little valid when practiced by a regularly drawn jury as when administered by one elected by a mob intent on death." This brave statement, insofar as Frank was concerned, was futile; indeed, he was lynched shortly afterward. But once more it suggests the temper of Hughes's mind.

Finally, in this brief discussion of Hughes's first term of service on the Court, a word should be said of his attitude towards the public interest as against the contract rights of the individual. The citadel of the latter is that clause of the federal Constitution which declares that no state shall pass any law impairing the obligation of contracts. This clause has been given a very extended application in the development of federal jurisprudence. It raises important questions in particular with regard to grants of franchises by the state authority to private persons. Are such grants to be interpreted liberally in favor of the individual, and a minimum of interference with them permitted? Or are they to be construed strictly, and nothing conceded that is not clearly given?

In general Hughes held to the latter view. In a railway case, for example, he insisted, in a dissent in which he associated himself with Justice Pitney, that the partial non-use of a franchise over a long term of years might work a revocation of the grant — with regard to what was not used. In a later case, where the facts were less complicated, he carried the whole Court with him in deciding that failure to exercise a grant is a ground for revocation or withdrawal. He again dissented, with three other justices, when the majority of the Court declared invalid as an impairment of the obligation of contract a city ordinance requiring a telephone company to remove its poles and wires from the streets unless it purchased a special franchise. He spoke for the whole Court, however, in deciding that regulatory rate legislation involved no violation of franchise rights, although the power to charge and collect tolls was included in the franchise. And he construed very strictly indeed, in two key cases, the grant of immunity from taxation made by a state to private individuals. Solicitude for the public interest, as opposed to individual interest, lay behind all these decisions.

There are a number of cases involving no direct constitutional issue, but merely the construction of a statute, which throw light on Hughes's mind and should be mentioned before we turn to other topics. For example, in construing the Food and Drug Act, aimed at misbranding, Hughes held, contrary to a majority of his colleagues, that the statute forbade not only misrepresentation with regard to the ingredients in a given article but also misrepresentation with regard to the curative properties of the same. In cases arising under the Sherman law, which forbade "combinations in restraint of trade," Hughes associated himself with the other members of the Court (except Justice Harlan) in reading the word "reasonable" into the act. But he was disposed to a critical view of monopolistic practice. In a series of decisions, he held against the right of a manufacturer to fix the prices at which his product might be sold by the wholesaler, the retailer, or other vendors; acting in dissent, he held that a patentee of a mimeographing machine could not require that only its own stencil paper, ink, and other supplies could be used with the machine itself; and he spoke for the Court in a third case in which the makers of a pharmaceutical product, Sanatogen, attempted to fix the price at which its product could be sold at retail. Such action, he declared, was contrary to the statute.

In all these cases there was a guiding principle. Hughes was never deeply theoretical in his view of the law. He addressed himself to the questions that came before him in a profoundly practical spirit. He was never captivated by words but always impressed by facts. The texture of his mind was precisely such as ought to be sought for in the administration of justice.

In the six years, 1910 to 1916, Hughes left a powerful impress upon the Court, especially through his masterly handling of the rate cases. Showing always a nice intellectual balance, he yet leaned towards the expansion of the powers of the federal government. On the question of the Fourteenth Amendment he again showed the truly judicial quality of his mind. In social and economic questions he was willing to give wider latitude than many other judges to the legislative authority of the states. But in the field of personal rights and of decent procedure he did not hesitate to participate in striking down state statutes which conflicted with what he deemed to be fundamental constitutional principles. His powerful mind and penetrating judgment established for him an enviable record as an Associate Justice of the United States.

Hughes was much admired by his brethren. Nothing could have been more complex than the railroad cases. It was a profound compliment that Chief Justice

White turned to a relatively new member of the Court to render judgment on that difficult problem. On the day when Hughes read his decision, Mrs. Hughes was in Court. Mr. Justice Day sent her a scribbled note which read, "Your husband has done a great work this day — the effect of which will be beneficially felt for generations to come." Justice Lurton wrote to her at the same time, "The opinion now being delivered is as able and important an opinion as any ever delivered from this Bench since the foundation of this Court." And the Chief Justice wrote to Hughes, "The country and Court owe you a debt they would have to go into bankruptcy if called upon to pay." It is noteworthy also that the two justices with whom he appears to have enjoyed the closest relations were the Chief Justice and Holmes. These were strong men, and Hughes appreciated strength. And, in the case of Holmes, the cordial and relaxed relations enjoyed by these two men, both in their way with a touch of austerity, are a charming example of judicial association. Holmes was perhaps the more brilliant; but Hughes was the more dynamic, with a greater faith and a deeper confidence in popular government.

Hughes's withdrawal from the Court to accept the presidential nomination, a subject for the next chapter, was the source of almost as many encomiums as his elevation to the bench. And the reason is not far to seek. He had identified himself, in virtually all of his important decisions, with the temper of the time. There is statesmanship, as well as precedent, in the judicial role. The process of social readjustment, never-ending as it is, can be much assisted by the Courts, acting, in Hughes's words, as "expert agencies of democracy expressing deliberate judgment under conditions essential to stability, and therefore in their proper action the necessary instrumentalities of progress." In this happy period, a period free from the stress of his Chief Justiceship, he acted with his colleagues, frequently with all of them, in giving to the interpretation of the Constitution that kind of flexibility, that adaptation to popular needs and to the spirit of the age that is the best guarantee of the high place the Supreme Court holds in the history and in the public regard of the American people.

III

The Campaign of 1916

From the supreme court, on which he served with such distinction, Hughes was, in 1916, precipitated into the maelstrom of national politics. His name had been raised as a possible presidential candidate more than once in *1912*, the year of the fierce intraparty quarrel between Theodore Roosevelt and William Howard Taft. The obvious man to heal the party breach was Hughes, not only because of his high character and reputation, but also because, as a judge on the bench, he had kept clear of the feud between the President and his predecessor. Indeed, just before the convention, Taft, writing to Hilles, the chairman of the Republican National Committee, indicated his willingness to withdraw from the fight if the former governor of New York could be nominated.

There could hardly have been a time, however, when the Republican presidential nomination was less to be desired. The Democrats, after sixteen years in opposition, had carried the Congress in 1910. The record of the Republicans under Taft had seriously shaken the prestige of the party in the country at large. And the violence of the preconvention campaign would, in and of itself, have come close to assuring defeat in the election struggle. Prudence alone (and Charles Evans Hughes was a prudent man) dictated an aloof attitude on his part.

When first approached, he firmly refused to allow his name to be used. And, as the days of the convention dawned, he went further. In June he issued a public statement through Rabbi Stephen Wise declaring that there was a question of principle involved. If judges could be taken from the bench to run for political office, the position of the judiciary itself might be weakened. Even in an extraordinary crisis, he declared, "no man is as essential to his country's well-being as is the unstained integrity of the courts." "I am informed," he later wrote to Root at the Republican convention, "that notwithstanding my published statement, efforts are being made to bring about my nomination. It should be understood, not only that this use of my name is unauthorized, but that, whatever the result, my decision will not be changed. The highest service that I can render in this difficult situation is to do all in my power to have it firmly established that a Justice of the Supreme Court is not avilable for political candidacy. The Supreme Court must be kept out of politics. I must add, to avoid all possible misunderstanding, that, even if nominated, I should decline."

Why did Hughes abandon in 1916 the principle he had laid down in 1912? The answer, since it involves complex questions of human motive, is not easy to state with finality. From the point of view of the party managers, his nomination was even more the answer to prayer than in 1912. A difficult campaign was ahead, with a strong Democratic President in office. The rift in the Republican Party could be healed in no better way than by nominating a man who had no political record whatsoever during the past four years, and who yet was a person of the highest ability and integrity. In intellectual and moral force Hughes stood head and shoulders above the time-serving politicians who might have aspired to the nomination. But why did he repudiate the declaration of 1912?

Hughes arrived at his decision only after the most painful reflection. His conduct in the winter and spring of 1916, when his name was being bandied about in connection with a possible nomination, was nothing less than impeccable. Not by so much as a gesture did he indicate that he had the slightest interest in the nomination. He tried definitely to keep away from those who sought to sound him out. "I am entirely out of politics," he wrote to C. Bascom Slemp of West Virginia in February of 1916. "I am totally opposed to the use of my name in connection with the nomination and selection or instruction of any delegates in my interest, either directly or indirectly." At no time did he make any kind of statement that could give encouragement to his backers.

Yet he was by no means sure where the path of duty lay. On the one hand was the principle he had laid down four years before. But, on the other, as he himself tells us, was the thought (a thought that had come to him many years before at the time of the gas investigation) that it was cowardly to shirk the call of duty. There were other considerations as well. Hughes, after all, was a Republican. Never a narrow partisan, he yet believed that the rehabilitation of his party was desirable in the interest of the nation, that the two-party system was one of America's most useful mechanisms in the operation of democratic government. He was critical, too, of the foreign policy of the administration. He believed that Wilson had fallen short of what was necessary in connection with preparedness for war. Possibly these judgments were not entirely objective. But there is no reason whatever to believe that they were not sincere.

Added to these considerations was the influence of his wife. The mutual devotion of the Hugheses was almost legendary. And Mrs. Hughes was convinced that if he received the nomination he had no right to refuse. Undoubtedly she urged him toward acceptance for, on one occasion, he exclaimed, "When you see me in my coffin, remember that I did not want to take this burden on myself."

Nothing but a sharp and categorical statement of abnegation could have arrested the movement for the Justice. The convention turned to him on the third ballot at Chicago. There were some dickerings with the remnants of the Progressive Party that Theodore Roosevelt had captained in 1912. The Rough Rider was not enthusiastic about the choice of Hughes. Indeed, he stultified his previous leadership by suggesting such well-known Tories as Henry Cabot Lodge and Leonard Wood. The Progressives themselves were, many of them, by no means anxious for any fusion with the Republicans, and eager to nominate their hero. Indeed, the Progressive convention ended by naming T.R. by acclamation and in an atmosphere of bitterness that boded ill for their cooperation with their foes of 1912. But Roosevelt refused to run and, as the political drama at Chicago came to an end, Hughes was at least certain that no third-party candidacy would mar his chances of election. As a matter of fact, the former President was to make many speeches for the Republican ticket in the course of the campaign.

The political conflict of 1916 is one of the most interesting in the history of the nation. Hughes entered it with some advantages that flowed from his six-year abstinence from politics, but these advantages were counterbalanced by serious handicaps. As we have already stated, the Justice had never been an organizing politician. He had made his way as governor of New York by sheer force of personality and of intelligence, and with the assistance of a dominant public mood. He needed badly for the direction of the campaign an experienced political tactician and strategist. Instead, exercising the usual prerogative of a presidential candidate to choose the chairman of the National Committee, he selected William R. Willcox, whom he had named to the Public Service Commission in New York City in 1907. The appointment was, beyond all question, a mistake. From the beginning to the end, the task of party organization was neglected. The local politicians constantly complained that they were ignored. If it be true, as many professionals believe, that elections are won in no small measure by the work in the precincts, there has rarely been a more ineptly conducted political conflict.

The handling of the press was also unskillful. The problem was a particularly difficult one in 1916, for, after all, the drama of a world war competed with the clash of the candidates for office. But instead of concentrating on the national audience in speeches that could be circulated throughout the country, Hughes's managers frittered him away in many speeches in small communities that hardly got reported at all — and this despite frequent protests and criticisms from some of his influential supporters.

Nor was the candidate himself effective, as he had been in the days of 1906 and 1908. He spoke earnestly, with his usual sense of order and with his usual somewhat heavy but by no means unattractive style. Though the conventional accusation of pussyfooting was directed against him, especially in dealing with the so-called hyphenate vote, a careful perusal of the *New York Times* for the months of September and October, 1916, does not suggest that he was at all wanting in sincerity. But on many of the issues which he chose to present to the voters, he was not able to take positions which carried the weight that was desirable. His campaign was mostly negative in character, critical rather than constructive, rarely elevated in tone, and rarely convincing as to future courses of action.

Take, for example, the question of Woodrow Wilson's policy towards the war in Europe. In the perspective of 1954, it would appear that a case could be made out for the view that American neutrality was a one-sided neutrality, always weighted in favor of the Allies. And it is even possible to argue (as this author emphatically would *not*) that Wilson, had he protested earlier and brought more pressure against Great Britain for her violations of international law, might have staved off the German retaliatory measure of the submarine campaign. But Hughes took the exactly opposite ground that the President had been remiss in not acting more vigorously against Germany. He excoriated the weakness of the Wilsonian policy; he sharply condemned what he described as the emollient attitude of the administration. There were difficulties in the logic of his position. For in May of 1916, under pressure from Washington, the Germans suspended the submarine campaign. In the fall of the year the President was in the position of one who had won a diplomatic victory (even if a victory that proved temporary) over the Reich.

There were inconsistencies, too, in what the Republican candidate had to say. One of the much-discussed incidents of the campaign was the sinking of the *Lusitania*. That vessel had been destroyed by a German submarine with the loss of over one hundred American lives in May of 1915. Wilson had riposted, not with war or with a severance of relations, but with a policy of note-writing, a policy which, as we have just seen, was temporarily successful. But in condemning this policy, Hughes, on one occasion, declared that had the administration been effective and strong, the vessel would not have been sunk at all, and, on another, that he would have severed relations when it *was* sunk. And he never indicated his understanding of the fact that in 1915 the country was by no means united with regard to the struggle in Europe, or prepared to take effective means for a policy based on force or the threat of force.

It was much the same with regard to the Mexican question, to which the Republican candidate returned again and again. Wilson's policy in Mexico was certainly not above criticism. Faced with a military *coup d'état* in Mexico City at the beginning of his term, he had declined to recognize the government of the "usurper," General Huerta, basing his refusal on moral grounds. He had been driven by his animosity to the dictator to order the occupation of Vera Cruz in April 1914, thus bringing the United States to the verge of war. He had extricated himself from this situation, it is true, by accepting the mediation of three of the Latin-American republics, but Mexico remained a plaguing problem throughout his first administration. Many offenses were committed against Americans in the revolutionary struggle that lasted till 1917, and there were even raids on the American border. The mission of General Pershing into Mexico, to catch the bandit Villa, undertaken against the protests of the government in Mexico City, had ended in a fiasco. The calling out of the National Guard to police the frontier had revealed the military weakness of the United States.

Yet in criticizing American policy towards Mexico (as indeed in criticizing American policy towards Germany), Hughes inevitably appeared as the champion of a policy that might lead to war. It was well enough to talk of the protection of American citizens, but how could these rights be protected short of armed intervention? Many Americans believed that American capitalists in Mexico ought themselves to bear the risks of their ventures as well as enjoy the high profits which they sought there. And there were undoubtedly others who did not wish to see embroilment to the south when the United States should keep its hands free to deal with the issues of the European war.

The Democratic politicians made great play, of course, of these considerations. From the very day that Woodrow Wilson was nominated at St. Louis, the cry was, "He kept us out of war." The cry was essentially disingenuous, since it seemed to convey not only praise for the past but a promise for the future — a promise no one could give. Wilson himself was honest enough to make it clear that he could guarantee nothing. But his supporters had found a good thing, and they made the most of it. There can be little doubt that the peace sentiment prevalent in much of the country contributed in a very substantial degree to the outcome of the election.

As the campaign proceeded, Hughes, in search of a domestic issue, emphasized more and more the tariff question. But the Underwood-Simmons bill, of the Wilson administration, was far from an extreme measure of reduction, and arguments for high protection in the midst of war could hardly be persuasive. Nor did Hughes's reasoning that at the end of the war Europe, exhausted and burdened with high taxes, would flood the American markets carry strong conviction with it. Indeed, on the tariff issue, as we have already said, Hughes was never at his best, and always at his most conventional.

One important issue came up in the campaign on which the Republican candidate took a strong and courageous stand. In September the railroad brotherhoods threatened to strike. The President called them to the White House and asked them to arbitrate their differences with the companies. But when they refused to do so, Wilson asked for the passage of a law which gave the men almost exactly what they wanted. Though in theory the so-called Adamson Act had to do with the length of the working day, it was actually a law providing the same wages for eight hours' work that had previously been paid for ten. This seemed to Hughes and to many other Americans an abandonment of principle in the face of a threat of coercion. The Republican candidate, in speech after speech, excoriated the action of the administration, and made it clear that he would have yielded nothing except after careful investigation of the facts in the dispute. His statements on this issue rang with deep conviction, and they were probably his most powerful attack upon the administration. It was all very well for Wilson to say that he had recommended the passage of the law because he thought the brotherhoods were right, but how could he be so sure? The only justification for his action, if any, would lie in the precarious international situation, and in the extreme danger of a strike at such a time. Hughes undeniably had a case for his criticism. Even here, however, there was a kind of negativism about his campaign. In the face of war prosperity, it was difficult to arouse the voters on the issue of a strike that had been averted.

There was also the constant irritant of factionalism in the Republican Party. There was a particularly virulent case of such factionalism in California, a state of great importance to the outcome. There the rift between the old-line Republicans and the Progressives remained unhealed. Hiram Johnson, the militant leader of the latter group, had left Chicago sore in spirit at Roosevelt's abandonment of the Progressive cause, and not ready to put his heart into the presidential campaign. Yet when Hughes came to the state, no real effort was made to propitiate Johnson, and the presidential party fell into the hands of the Old Guard. Hughes refused to take sides in the state campaign, feeling that such action would be undignified and perhaps also that it might cost him votes in the East. He deeply wounded the sensitive ego of the Progressive leader. The climax of a series of errors came when the presidential candidate and Johnson, who was running for the Senate, were for a little while in the same hotel at Long Branch. The Californian refused to take the initiative — as in courtesy he might well have done — in bringing about a meeting. Hughes himself was carefully kept away from the Progressive leader, and when, back in Los Angeles, he discovered his error, it was too late to atone for it. The ruffled pride of Johnson refused to be satisfied.

The position of Theodore Roosevelt was also a problem. It was quite impossible to dispense with T.R.'s support. Yet the former President handicapped the candidate in several ways. He seemed to be talking for war rather than for Hughes, and he could not be repressed. In addition, he had alienated many of his former followers by his desertion of the standard he had raised in 1912. And it is not impossible that the very violence of his language and his vitriolic hatred of Wilson may actually have strengthened the President.

Finally, there was the Billion Dollar Special, a woman's campaign train under the sponsorship of such persons as Mrs. Payne Whitney, Mrs. Cornelius Vanderbilt, and Mrs. Elizabeth Stotesbury. In the West especially, where women voted, the spectacle of these Eastern women of wealth advising them as to their choice was not calculated to win friends or to influence people.

The campaign was nevertheless a very close one. Wilson's victory in 1912 had been the victory of a minority candidate. The country was still, as it had been since 1896, preponderantly Republican. The powerful support of the business interests of the East was largely enlisted behind Hughes. When election day dawned, November 6, it seemed probable that the President would be defeated.

Indeed, as the returns came in on that Tuesday evening, they were so favorable to the challenger that many persons, clustered before the bulletin boards and screens, went home early in the belief that the election had been decided. The *New York Times,* which had backed Wilson, actually conceded the victory to his opponent.

But with Wednesday morning came a different story. In the East the Republicans had won a remarkable victory; almost every state north of Mason and Dixon's Line had gone down the line for Hughes. But in the West the situation was far different. Beyond the Great River a veritable flood of votes in what was traditionally Republican territory was cast for the President. The Western farmers, to whom the war had brought great prosperity, voted in droves for Wilson. By the end of the day it was clear that the decision would be made final only with the returns from California. And these returns were delayed; in the mountain counties in 1916 communication was still slow and difficult. Never since 1876 had the nation been in such suspense. It was Friday morning before the last ballots had been counted. Then it was discovered that California had gone for the President by a plurality in the neighborhood of 3000, and that Wilson had been re-elected.

Because the final and decisive returns came from the West Coast, an exaggerated importance has sometimes been given to this feature of the result. There are other ways of interpreting the election. Wilson won by 277 electoral votes against 254. East of the Mississippi and north of the Potomac he had carried only Ohio and New

Hampshire. Without Ohio, with its twenty-four electoral votes, he would have been beaten. It is probable that the railroad workers' vote in that state, won by the passage of the Adamson law, was, as truly as the California imbroglio, the determining factor in his election. One can go at the matter in another way. A shift in three small states, New Hampshire (carried by fewer than 100 votes), North Dakota (carried by fewer than 2000 in a total vote of more than 100,000), and New Mexico or Arizona, would have resulted in a Republican victory.

It is worth noting, however, that Hughes was defeated in the popular vote as well as in the electoral college. He did not suffer the fate of Grover Cleveland in 1888, who had a popular plurality and yet failed to win as a result of our peculiar mechanism for the election of a President.

The campaign of 1916 was perhaps the least happy episode in Hughes's brilliant and useful career. His own most ardent supporters said this at the time. It may be that he suffered from the outset from a kind of self-contradiction. He could hardly have been entirely satisfied with his reversal as to the duty of a Supreme Court judge. He lacked the intense partisan spirit that often makes a man effective on the stump. He was able to make men admire him, but he did not have the warmth to move masses of men to follow him as a leader blindly. He knew nothing, we must repeat, of the arts of organization politics. More important than all this, in attempting to unify the Republican Party, he inevitably affronted — or at least failed to attract — the progressive elements which had left the Republican Party in 1912, and which saw in him in 1916 no sign of the liberal leader of a decade before. There was much force in the view of Frederick Davenport, one of his devoted followers, who wrote many years afterwards that the presidential campaign was a lapse in his greatness. There was force, too, in the commentary of John Palmer Gavit, who in an article entitled "What Hughes Was This?" sharply criticized his bearing in the campaign.

It is, however, a measure of Hughes's size as a public man that never at any time after the result was known did he give way either to bitterness or to public lamentation. Indeed, in the philosophic calm of later years he asked himself the question whether, in view of the war into which the United States was soon plunged, Wilson was not more able to unite the country than he would have been. And he rallied heartily to the support of the President when war came.

With his defeat in 1916, Hughes returned to the practice of law. Characteristically, he refused many attractive offers. He felt that he must maintain his independence and therefore returned to his old firm. From the outset he was swamped with business. But despite heavy professional burdens he subordinated his private interests and the opportunity to make money to his instinct for public service. He was for some time chairman of the District Draft Appeals Board for New York City, and did a staggering amount of work in this job. At a later date he was requested by President Wilson to investigate the situation in the aircraft industry, and he rendered a report which was accepted by the Attorney General as authoritative.

As a lawyer, Hughes played a part in two conspicuous questions before again entering public office.

The first of these, which brought upon Hughes much criticism, was the famous Newberry case. Truman H. Newberry had been Roosevelt's Secretary of the Navy. In 1918 he was a candidate for Senator in the Republican primaries in the state of Michigan against Henry Ford. The campaign was bitterly contested, and won only by the lavish use of money on the part of Newberry's friends, with or without his knowledge. He was convicted under the Federal Corrupt Practices Act of 1910, which severely restricted campaign expenditures with regard to the nomination and election of members of the House and Senate. Hughes did not participate in the original trial, but he argued Newberry's appeal before the Supreme Court of the United States. The result was an acquittal, though the justices disagreed as to the grounds. Hughes had argued that the regulation of primary elections by the Congress was unconstitutional, and that it did not flow, as the Government argued, from the congressional right to regulate elections. In this contention he was sustained by only five justices. But the other four found for the defendant on the ground that Newberry was not personally implicated in the expenditure of the excessive sums disbursed in the primary campaign. In a sense, then, the judgment was unanimous.

There are, however, several questions to be raised with regard to Hughes's part in this episode. He doubtless believed Newberry to be unjustly accused, and assumed his defense on that ground. But it seems curious that a jurist so generally favorable to the extension of national power should have resorted to a dubious constitutional argument as to the validity of a statute in order to secure his client's acquittal. It is also true that he was put in the position (a position which he surely would have repudiated) of defending lavish expenditures in politics. It is open to a lawyer (and this ought to be not only understood but underlined) to argue any case on the basis of the law and of the law alone. But on grounds of broad public policy it seems strange that Hughes would identify himself with this particular case. And it is not extraordinary that his enemies suggested that he was moved by a narrow partisanship that was by no means natural to him.

His reaction was more characteristic in the famous case of the expulsion of five Socialist members of the New York Assembly in January of 1920. A foreign observer might find curious the contradiction in the American character which consists, on the one hand, in a high degree of common sense and the inveterate habit of compromise in American politics and, on the other hand, in the extraordinary verbal violence and intolerance which sometimes sweep the nation. There is probably no country in which violent social upheaval is and has been less likely than the United States. Yet there are few in which there have been more extraordinary demonstrations of antagonism not only to revolutionary change but even to programs of reform that challenge the basic assumptions of the business order. Perhaps this very intensity is, from one angle of vision, a manifestation of faith, of a faith not altogether without value. But at times it threatens the very democratic order which it assumes to protect. From the time of the Alien and Sedition Acts to the time of Senator McCarthy sporadic outbursts of feeling in this land have gone far beyond the necessities of self-protection and involve fundamental problems of American ideals.

There was particular reason for such an outburst in 1919 and 1920, when, added to the sense of national self-confidence that came with victory, there was presented to the American people for the first time the spectacle of a revolutionary order which challenged the assumptions of their way of life. There had been enough unrest at the end of the conflict to unsettle the nerves of jittery conservatives: there had been a number of bombing outrages, including the bombing of the house of A. Mitchell Palmer, Attorney General of the United States; the May Day parades of 1919 had resulted in much street fighting in Boston and in Cleveland; there had been a clash of obscure origin, but of widespread notice, in Centralia, Washington, which had resulted in the death of four servicemen and the lynching of one other. In response to these events Attorney General Palmer had responded with action more vigorous than judicious, with raids that violated constitutional principles and indiscriminate arrests. The country was in a troubled mood as the year 1920 opened.

Then came the action of the Republican leadership in the New York State Assembly. In the election of the preceding year five Socialist members had been legally and regularly elected from the City of New York. At the beginning of the 1920 session they were permitted to take their seats and for about two hours actually participated in the transaction of business. Then, without a word of warning, they were hauled before the Speaker, soundly lectured, informed that they would be excluded from all legislative business pending investigation, and then escorted from the chamber by the sergeant-at-arms.

In the face of this kind of thing many respectable men kept silent, and many others were confused. The Socialist Party leaders had opposed the war; the Socialist Party doctrines were suggestive of possibly drastic changes in American society. It might well have been the case that no clear and strong voice would be raised to challenge the action of the Assembly leaders. But the clear and strong voice was raised; and it was the voice of Charles Evans Hughes. Almost immediately he protested to Speaker Sweet. His protest went to the heart of the matter. "Are Socialists unconvicted of crime," he wrote, "to be denied the ballot? If Socialists are permitted to vote, are they not permitted to vote for their own candidates? If their candidates are elected and are men against whom, as individuals, charges of disqualifying offenses cannot be laid, are they not entitled to their seats? . . . I understand that it is said that the Socialists constitute a combination to overthrow the Government. The answer is plain. If public officers or private citizens have any evidence that any individuals, or group of individuals, are plotting revolution and seeking by violent measures to change our Government, let the evidence be laid before the proper authorities and swift action be taken for the protection of the community. Let every resource of inquiry, of pursuit, of prosecution be employed to ferret out and punish the guilty according to our laws. But I count it a most serious mistake to proceed, not against individuals charged with violation, but against masses of our citizens combined for political action, by denying them the only resource of peaceful government; that is, action by the ballot box and through duly elected representatives in legislative bodies."

This classical statement struck no responsive chord in the breast of Speaker Sweet, but it was only the beginning of Hughes's fight for what he considered fundamental principle. He took the lead in securing action from the bar association of New York City and from the state bar association condemning the action of the Assembly. It is a rather melancholy fact that, strong as was his position and great as was his intellectual and moral influence, it was only by a vote of 131 to 100 that the city bar approved the motion to appoint a committee to argue the case at Albany. Nor was the attitude of the state lawyers as unequivocal as one might have hoped. In the face of the challenge the members of the legal profession blew both hot and cold.

Hughes failed to make his view prevail at Albany. Indeed, his committee was refused a hearing. He had to satisfy himself with filing a brief in which he excoriated the lawmakers in no uncertain terms. He declared that to require the Socialist members to prove their right to be seated was "a reversal of the rule applicable to the meanest criminal." He described the Assembly action as reminiscent of the English state trials of the sixteenth and seventeenth centuries. He scored what he called heresy hunting in no uncertain terms.

The politicians at Albany, however, had gone too far to retreat. Obedient to the immemorial political principle that one must never confess error, they stuck to their guns. They not only expelled the Socialists; they passed a law outlawing the Socialist Party. They scorned the advice and repudiated the viewpoint of the man who was by now, by all odds, the most distinguished Republican in the United States.

It is not easy to measure the effects of Hughes's action. In the early months of 1920, there were still many evidences of persecution and hysteria. It seems exaggerated to attribute to Hughes's courageous statement the principal role in the turning of the tide. But, whether this be true or not, he had erected a standard to which the faithful friends of the democratic process might repair. When all too many were silent, he had spoken out in behalf of a traditional American ideal.

IV

The League Fight

THERE ARE FEW EPISODES in the history of American foreign policy more intriguing than the fight over the League of Nations and the Treaty of Versailles in 1919 and 1920. In this fight Charles Evans Hughes inevitably played a part; and, when the struggle was over, it rested with him in no small degree to determine how the United States should reconcile its aspirations towards international cooperation with the exigencies of practical politics. Years after the event, the struggle still has, for those who witnessed it, a peculiar poignancy and all the elements of high drama.

And that struggle remained relevant to the issues of foreign policy more than three decades later. For at the core of the conflict lay that idea of collective security which was to figure so largely in the political language of the future. It will be worthwhile to try to set the whole matter in some kind of historical perspective before turning to the story of the battle itself.

The idea of collective action for the preservation of peace, insofar as the United States is concerned, occurs as early as Theodore Roosevelt's Nobel-peace-prize address in 1910. But it was the World War that gave it greater currency and led to the establishment of a nonpartisan organization, the League to Enforce Peace, to propagandize for an international association of the nations which would act on the principle of common action against an aggressor state. Wilson cautiously adopted the idea in his speech to the League in May of 1916, and saw that a plank endorsing it was inserted in the Democratic platform of that year.

The involvement of the United States in the World War increased his conviction of the necessity of some such principle. America, he reasoned, could never again be neutral in a large-scale conflict. It was necessary, therefore, to concert measures to prevent such a conflict, and the way to do this was through the acceptance of the obligation of collective action against an aggressor. Wilson went to Paris after the defeat of Germany to secure the acceptance of this concept, got it incorporated in the treaty of Versailles, and came home to fight for its acceptance in the United States. The great partisan battle of 1919 and 1920 followed.

We shall not be able to approach this struggle with objectivity unless we look beyond 1919 to 1954. The principle of collective security, in its *universal* application, was not accepted in 1920 or later. It may never be accepted in the future. To get *everybody* to combine against *any* aggressor is a very large order, and it assumes that states will be actuated by a fundamental concern for peace rather than by a concern for their own interests.

Yet the idea has shown remarkable vitality. Rejected in 1919 and 1920 in America, it was accepted in the Charter of the United Nations in 1945. While perhaps impracticable as a universal principle, by its emphasis on the immorality of aggressive war it has contributed substantially to the actual shaping of policy. In particular it has made easier the transition of the United States from isolationism to a policy of association and alliance. Had this nation accepted its implications earlier, the bloody history of the 1940s might conceivably have run a different course.

In the actual train of events in 1919 and 1920, Wilson made his own success and the conversion of the American people to his point of view about as difficult as he could. He exacerbated the spirit of partisanship by his appeal for a Democratic Congress in 1918. On October 30, criticizing this appeal, Charles Evans Hughes uttered words that might well have been heeded in the White House but were not.

Speaking at the Union League Club, he said, "If the President stood before the world only as party leader, his influence would be slight indeed. His just influence is based on the extent to which he fully represents the sentiment of this nation regardless of party. He will not be the effective spokesman of the nation unless through consultation and deliberation with those who represent the thought of the nation he can be said to express strongly preponderating if not unanimous sentiment." Fundamentally, whatever the nobility of Wilson's ideals, we must concede that this point of view was sound. We may say, if we will, that the President was acting on a theory, a theory very dear to him, the theory of responsible party government. But the party system in the United States was not what it was in Britain, Wilson's model; and the requirement of a two-thirds vote of the Senate for the ratification of treaties made consultation of the opposition indispensable. It is possible to understand, but it is difficult to defend, the President's appeal.

The partisan spirit with regard to the treaty was further stimulated by the composition of the delegation that went to Paris to make peace. As far back as 1898, President McKinley, smooth-practicing politician that he was, had sought to ensure favorable action on the treaty of peace with Spain by putting a Democratic Senator on the peace commission. Yet, in 1919, in a much more difficult situation, Wilson chose a delegation with no Republican representation except for Henry White, a career diplomat without political influence. There were understandable reasons for not choosing Henry Cabot Lodge, the prospective chairman of the committee on foreign relations, for his venomous hatred of the President was well known. But was it impossible to choose *any* Republican of weight? Might not Hughes himself have been selected?

However this may be, the President went to Paris determined to fight for a League of Nations. In the evening sessions of February, 1919, there was struck off the first draft of what was to become the Covenant. The text was published and soon became a matter of lively debate in the United States.

Amongst the criticisms of the projected document, criticisms in which Hughes was to join, was the famous Article X, which was to become the crux of the ensuing battle. This Article read as follows: "The members of the League agree to respect and preserve as against external aggression the territorial integrity and existing political independence of the Members of the League. In case of any such aggression or in case of any threat or danger of such aggression, the Council shall advise upon the means by which this obligation shall be fulfilled."

From the beginning Hughes objected to this provision. He disliked it when he first read it. On March 7 he made a slanting allusion to it in an interview in which he said, "We are all for anything that will assure" permanent peace, "but in an effort to bring about world peace we must not involve ourselves in a League of Nations that may make us the pawn of selfish people in other lands, and in the end destroy the peace and happiness of our own people." On March 30 he analyzed the Covenant at length in a speech before the Union League Club. Once again he turned to Article X. "I regard this guaranty," he said, "as a trouble-breeder and not a peace-maker . . . its inflexibility should condemn it. . . . The guaranty makes no allowance for changes which may be advisable. It ascribes a prescience and soundness of judgment to the present Peace Conference in erecting States and defining boundaries which no body in the history of the world has ever possessed. . . . It gives no fair opportunity for adjustments. It is in the teeth of experience. . . . What good reason is there for a guaranty to apply to unknown and unforeseeable contingencies? Why not leave the future to conference and decision in the light of events?"

This point of view is entirely intelligible. But we should make no mistake about its import. It denied the validity of the principle of collective security, a principle in which Hughes was never really interested. He had given a kind of lip service to it in his acceptance speech of 1916. But his considered view of the League was probably most clearly expressed in a letter which he wrote some months later to Senator Hale. "There is plain need for a League of Nations," he said, "in order to provide for the adequate development of international law, for creating and maintaining organs of international justice and machinery of conciliation and conference and for giving effect to measures of international cooperation which from time to time may be agreed upon." Not a word, it will be observed, about common international action against an aggressor, not a word about the sovereign principle to which President Wilson attached so much importance.

Granted Hughes's initial point of view, was it necessary to attack Article X so vigorously? This is an interesting question. "It is a serious thing," he said in the speech from which we have just quoted, "to enter into an engagement unless there is reason to believe that Congress will act accordingly." Of course it is. But Article X stated that "the Council will advise as to the means by which this obligation shall be fulfilled." Was it not possible, therefore, in all candor to interpret this article as requiring something less than full-scale war? Was it not possible to read into it a moral condemnation of aggression, to serve as the basis of full-scale punitive action on the part of the states most interested, and of something less than this on the part of other states, binding the latter to measures of disapproval far short of war? As a matter of fact, the Covenant laid comparatively little emphasis on the sanction of arms. Article XVI, which deals with the action to be taken against an aggressor, sets forth economic measures of reprisal in some detail. But with regard to the use of force there is only the mild provision, "It shall be the duty of the Council in such case to recommend to the several Governments concerned what effective military, naval or air force the Members of the League shall severally contribute to the armed forces to be used to protect the Covenants of the League."

Nor was it quite right to assume that Article X involved the freezing of the status quo. It prohibited the alteration of the status quo by war and, perhaps, by internal subversion, but it did no more. This prohibition may have been unwise, and it certainly did not prevent great changes from taking place before two decades had gone by. But it did not prevent the peaceful adjustment of territorial questions by "conference and decision," to use Hughes's own words.

Furthermore the language of Article X did not prevent all the other signatories of the treaty, and most of the nations of the world, from adhering to the Covenant. And in any case, Hughes himself was ready to accept a reservation to the Article which did no more than assert that

Congress must be the judge of the conditions under which it applied. Logically, if he felt the whole principle unsound, he should at all times have insisted upon its elimination from the League draft.

In the Union League Club speech of March 30, in addition to his criticisms of Article X, Hughes made other suggestions with regard to the Covenant. He proposed numerous changes and spoke out for modifications of the Paris draft. He suggested, for example, that domestic questions, such as the tariff and immigration, be excluded from League consideration, and that these two specific matters be mentioned explicitly. He also declared that the text of the document should make clear that no American territory should be acquired by any foreign power, and that all exclusively American questions should be settled by the American nations alone. He made these proposals, it is only fair to say, while there was still time to alter the text of the instrument (which was indeed reconsidered by the Conference Committee in April), and doubtless with a sincere desire to see the document accepted and duly ratified.

At Paris, President Wilson pressed forward with the Covenant. It would not be right to say that he took no account of the criticism at home. But he certainly did not go so far as the situation demanded. He stood pat on Article X. With regard to the Monroe Doctrine he fought for the insertion in the Covenant of an Article which described it, most ambiguously, as a "regional understanding" unaffected by the general prescriptions of the document. With regard to domestic questions he secured the acceptance of a principle which permitted the Council to decide what constituted such a question. It was a foregone conclusion that none of these modifications would satisfy the rapidly growing partisan opposition in the United States.

During the spring, for the most part Hughes abstained from public discussion. But in July he gave his views in a letter to Senator Hale. There had to be reservations to the treaty to protect the just interests of the United States. But how should these reservations be treated? President Wilson insisted at all times that they be divorced from the treaty itself. Ex-President Taft was not averse to this point of view. In the Senate, on the other hand, there was a powerful minority sentiment in favor of actually amending the instrument. Hughes took a position taken by no other important public figure. He declared in the first place, "It is manifest that attempted reservations will be ineffectual unless they qualify the act of ratification. The adoption of resolutions by the Senate setting forth its views will not affect the obligation of the Congress if it is in fact ratified without reservations which constitute a part of the instrument of ratification." But he went on to say, "Where there is simply a statement of interpretation based by the ratifying power upon ambiguous clauses of the treaty, whether or not the statement is called reservations, the case is really not one of amendment, and acquiescence of the other parties may readily be inferred unless express objection is made after notice has been received." He proceeded to suggest interpretative reservations of the type he had proposed before.

His advice was not taken. The Senate, partly under the

influence of partisan feeling, went much further. It increased the number of the reservations and it required that they be accepted by three out of four of the principal ratifying powers. President Wilson refused to accept the treaty in this form. He advised his followers to vote against it, and in November, 1919, it went down to defeat.

Thereafter Hughes played little part in the treaty struggle. Whether or not the treaty, in the shape in which it was finally acted upon, should have been accepted by President Wilson is a question on which men will divide for a long time to come. It is possible to argue that, in its mutilated form, it could not have proved acceptable to our principal associates in the war. In one respect, the reservation on Article X, as adopted by the Senate, encroached seriously on the presidential prerogative. But many of the stoutest admirers of Wilson have felt more than a twinge of regret at the unyielding attitude which made him unwilling at least to try to see what could be done with the treaty in its altered form. And more critical historians have judged him very harshly indeed.

The violent partisan battle over the League was projected into the campaign of 1920. Since Hughes had taken a position which identified him with at least one element of his party, it seems strange that no one brought his name forward in connection with the presidential nomination. He certainly made no attempt to push himself. He would seem to have been an excellent choice. He had barely been defeated in 1916. The tactical errors of four years before could have been readily corrected, and in any case, the country was clearly drifting away from the administration. He was intellectually — with the possible exception of Root, now an old man — the most powerful Republican in the country. Yet no voice was raised in his behalf. Perhaps the explanation is that Hughes had always been something less than beloved by the professional politicians. And this was a professional politicians' year. Out of the smoke-filled rooms at Chicago came the nomination of Warren Gamaliel Harding for the Presidency of the United States.

We do not know Hughes's initial reactions to this nomination. But on August 25 he went to Marion and there delivered himself in praise of the Republican candidate. "We want a man of courage," he said, "possessing a sound common sense, who has an appreciation of American institutions, and who knows how to conduct great affairs in accordance with the spirit of our institutions. We want one who will give us a high standard of administration. We want someone who will take account of the great obligations of the most resourceful people in the world, and enter upon the performance of these obligations and carry them out successfully in a manner consonant with the maintenance of national security. Such a man is Senator Harding." This description of the Senator was hardly to be vindicated by events.

In the campaign that followed, Hughes played a part, but not a conspicuous part. When he spoke on the League, he was apt to stress the issue of Article X. The essentials of a League, he declared in a press statement on August 26, were the creation of an international court, of agencies of conciliation and conference. Again no word of collective action against aggression. On September 19 he described the attacks on the Senate reservationists as "puerile and unworthy," and declared by implication that the Covenant as drafted did not concert with American principles, or secure the preservation of peace. On September 23, in the notification ceremonies for Nathan Miller, Republican candidate for governor of New York, he spoke of "the surrender of American principles and interests," of the Democratic "policy of delusion," of the danger of "fatuously committing ourselves to a broad undertaking, pledging the use of national arms in unknown contingencies regardless of our opinion at the time of the merits of the controversy." But he was, certainly, far removed from the point of view of the irreconcilable Republicans who were anxious to scrap the League altogether. There is indeed some reason to believe, both from the phraseology and the emphases, that it was he who drafted the famous appeal of the thirty-one Republicans, issued on October 15, to vote for Senator Harding in order to bring the United States into the world organization. This statement began with a severe belaboring of Article X, in terms that strongly suggest the Hughes point of view. It sustained the position of the Senate in attempting to qualify the obligations of the Covenant by reservations. It declared that the ratification of the treaty was impossible without such reservations. But it went on to say that the Republican Party was "bound by every consideration of honor and good faith" to bring the country into the League. Besides Hughes many other distinguished Republicans signed the declaration.

The victory of the Republicans in the campaign of 1920 was overwhelming. And when the smoke cleared away, Hughes found himself once more invited to participate in public life. The President-elect called him to Marion within a month of the election and, perhaps on this occasion, offered him the post of Secretary of State. At any rate, when the President's Cabinet was announced, just before the inauguration, the New Yorker's name stood at the head of the list.

The role that Hughes played as Secretary of State will call for detailed analysis in this study. But with regard to the question of the League it may be worthwhile if we pursue here the story of his attitude to the end of the Harding-Coolidge administration.

There is not the slightest doubt that the round robin of the thirty-one was written with a sincere purpose. Perhaps a thoroughly objective view would have suggested that since, in the League fight, the so-called Republican irreconcilables had opposed the Covenant in any form or guise, it would be difficult to command their support in case of a Republican victory, and that every consideration of party loyalty and party cohesion would dictate a cautious line of action with regard to the Treaty of Versailles. But the signers of the famous declaration, the new Secretary among them, had not perceived this.

On entering office, Hughes soon became aware of the difficulties that lay ahead. Senators Borah and Johnson and the rest of the "battalion of death" stood square athwart his path. The President himself had no stomach for a fight.

The crashing majorities for the Republican ticket, after the Democratic effort to make the League the central issue of the campaign, seemed to indicate that the American public were at least lukewarm on the issue. Indeed, in the retrospect of history, it seems safe to say that the complexities of the problem, or even the guiding principles of the debate, were by no means thoroughly understood by the voters. The American electorate hardly grasped the issue of collective security in 1920.

In the face of the practical situation, and only after he had more than once pressed upon the President affirmative action on an altered treaty with reservations, Hughes decided that he would have to abandon the Versailles Treaty and steer affairs in the direction of a separate peace with Germany.

His determination to move along this line was based on purely practical considerations. The alternative was resignation, resignation before his work had hardly begun, and in circumstances particularly embarrassing. He believed, as he was later to write to George Wickersham, that if a fight had been made, it would have failed. In this he may have been rationalizing his own decision. He was, after all, a party man, and the idea of a battle at the outset of his service could not have been very attractive to him. Consistency was less important than the opportunity for public service. He made his decision and kept to himself the doubts and disappointments, if there were any, that may have assailed him.

In retrospect, the determination to abandon the League

treaty seems less fundamental than it seemed to the passionate advocates of international cooperation in 1921. Essentially, though there was doubtless in the United States a genuine and widespread desire to participate in an international organization, there was, as we have said, very little understanding or acceptance of the principle of collective security on which Woodrow Wilson's advocacy of the Covenant had been based. The struggle over Article X, in which Hughes had played a part, was not a mere matter of semantics. It involved the important question of whether the United States would commit itself wholeheartedly to collective action for the maintenance of peace; and this question, in the Senate debates, had been decided in the negative. The dropping of the treaty, moreover, left the way still open, in 1922, for cooperation with the League if the members of that organization sought to carry out the prescriptions of the Covenant.

Yet Hughes's abandonment of the stand he had taken the year before roused much resentment. This resentment was increased by the fact that for a time, apparently due to the oversight or churlishness of a subordinate official, League communications remained unanswered at Washington, giving the impression of cool indifference to the experiment in international cooperation being instituted at Geneva. There were, too, more practical reasons for criticizing the wisdom of the Secretary's decision. The Treaty of Versailles called for American representation on the Reparations Commission which was to estimate the extent of Germany's liability to the Allies for the damages they had sustained in the war, and it was confidently expected that the American member would be chairman, and would exercise a decisive and, in all probability, a moderating influence in dealing with this important problem. By abandoning the treaty, this advantage of position was surrendered, and when Hughes came to negotiate a separate peace with Germany, he found it impossible to correct the difficulty. The consequences were unfortunate and diminished gravely the weight of the United States in a question in which it had an important interest.

Just how seriously Hughes estimated his own defeat on the treaty issue is impossible to say. He was an extraordinarily discreet man and rarely gave way to public lamentation. He was, also, if one may judge from the pages of his diary, very rarely dissatisfied with his major decisions in the State Department. But there was a distinction between his attitude towards the League when questions of collective security were involved and his attitude when nothing more than international cooperation for the promotion of desirable ends or the judicial settlements of international disputes was concerned.

In the early 1920s, there were several efforts to translate the principle of collective security into terms more precise and more effective than those of the Covenant. The first was the Draft Treaty of Mutual Assistance of 1923. This treaty permitted the Council of the League, in case of the outbreak of hostilities, to designate the aggressor nation, and obligated the contracting parties to furnish each other mutual assistance against the aggressing state. It assumed that such aid should be both military and economic. It limited the operation of sanctions by declaring that in principle no state would be required to assist in military, naval, or air operations outside the continent in which the aggression had taken place. This treaty was communicated not only to the members of the League, but to the United States.

Hughes responded in extremely chilly fashion. "In view of the constitutional organization of this Government, and in view of the fact that the United States is not a member of the League of Nations, this Government would find it impossible to give its adherence." This reply itself was not decisive. It is doubtful whether the Draft Treaty would in any case have been adopted. The attitude of the United States did not alone wreck a project that was on the verge of acceptance. Yet the answer went further than was necessary, and further than the accepted practice of the government at a later date. For it seemed to say that the Executive could not enter into an engagement which bound the United States to common action with other states. Hughes's comment on the "constitutional organization of this Government" would, if accepted, rule out many later agreements. It revealed him as taking a narrow and, perhaps one may say, a shortsighted view of the future.

Still more drastic was the Secretary's attitude towards the Geneva protocol of 1924. This document, an attempt on the part of European diplomats at improving the machinery for collective security, erected an elaborate system for the pacific settlement of international disputes, defined aggression with more precision than had the Covenant, and again inserted a saving clause declaring that sanctions should be applied "in the degree which the geographical position and particular situation [of each state] allows." It was unanimously approved by the Fifth Assembly of the League on October 2, 1924, at a meeting at which were present such important statesmen as Ramsay MacDonald, prime minister of Great Britain, and Edouard Herriot, premier of the French Republic. Though the fall of the Labor government shortly after altered the situation, it by no means assured that the protocol would be shelved.

Yet when Sir Esmé Howard, in the winter of 1925, sounded Mr. Hughes as to the American attitude, and in language that suggested a sympathetic attitude on the part of the British Government, the Secretary responded in terms highly critical and discouraging. He spoke of the Geneva document as implying "a proposal of a concert against the United States," flatly stated that the application of sanctions against another state might be "inimical to American trade" and that "there was one thing he believed could be depended upon, and that was that this Government from its very beginning had been insistent upon the rights of neutrals and would continue to maintain them." He added that "he did not believe that any Administration, short of a treaty concluded and ratified, could commit the country against assertion of its neutral rights in case there should be occasion to demand their recognition." And, in addition to these comments, he seemed to suggest that the British sounding was a mere excuse for inaction on the part of the British Government. Three days later, after a conversation with the President, he reasserted his point of view.

We cannot assess with any accuracy the weight to be given to these comments of the Secretary so far as the final failure of the protocol is concerned. But they revealed very clearly Hughes's unsympathetic attitude towards the idea of collective security. He was under no especial political pressure in January 1925. The Coolidge administration had easily been returned to power. His statements to Sir Esmé not only rejected that idea but implied that American policy would resist the application of sanctions if the experiment were tried.

If Hughes took a critical view of the principle of united action for the maintenance of peace, he was by no means hostile to the League idea as an agency of international cooperation or to the collateral agency which the League had created, the World Court. His respect for law led him to take a keen interest in the international adjudication of international disputes. Large sections of American public opinion were no doubt in accord with him on this point. Indeed, there had been in the United States an exaggerated belief in the possibility of settling international controversies by legal means. Until it was finally laid to rest for a decade in 1935, the whole problem of

American adhesion to the World Court protocol was given a wholly disproportionate importance in the discussion of American foreign policy. The friends of the League attributed to it a symbolic importance; the enemies of the League were not slow to take the same view.

At the outset of his administration of the State Department, the Secretary took an extremely cautious position on this matter. The protocol creating the Court (a protocol in the drafting of which no less distinguished an American than Elihu Root had played a part) called for the nomination of the judges by the representatives of the various states on the old Hague tribunal, or rather by the national panels from which the judges of that tribunal could be drawn. Election was to take place by the vote of the Assembly and the Council of the League. When the first occasion for nominations arose, Mr. Root, as the senior member of the American panel, sounded Mr. Hughes as to the propriety of putting forward any candidates. The Secretary responded with extreme caution and yet with some subtlety. He declared that he had no request to make; at the same time he indicated that compliance with the League's request "would involve serious risk of immediate controversy which might be very injurious to the success of the important policies the government is now pursuing." The hint was taken; in the face of the refusal of the Hague panel to act, the Secretary stated, with something less than complete ingenuousness, that the "American Hague judges acted in accordance with their own views of propriety." This episode took place in the fall of 1921.

It is perhaps not surprising that the Secretary was cautious. He was at the time engaged in preparations for the great conference on reduction of armaments which was to bulk so large in the achievements of his administration. He was acting from what he believed to be a sound sense of timing. But as the months passed, he found it possible to take a stronger position. In October of 1922 he announced that he believed that suitable arrangements could be made for the participation by the American Government in the election of judges. And by next February he succeeded in overcoming the indolence or the indifference of President Harding. On the twenty-fourth of that month he dictated a long letter which was accepted by the Chief Executive and which was sent to the Senate, recommending American ratification with reservations of the World Court protocol.

By suggesting four conditions and understandings to be made a part of the instrument of adhesion Hughes hoped to stave off unfavorable reactions in the Senate. It was to be declared that American action involved no commitment with regard to the League; that the United States should take part in the proceedings of the Council and Assembly with regard to the election of judges; that the American share of the expenses of the Court should be fixed by Congress; and that the Court statute should not be amended without the consent of the United States.

A more innocent proposal could hardly have been imagined. The Court was a court of voluntary jurisdiction. The Secretary, in later correspondence with Senator Lodge, made it perfectly clear that the American Government had no intention whatsoever of submitting to any compulsory jurisdiction, such as could be arranged by signing an additional protocol. All that was involved was participation in an institution that had already been established, that was actually functioning, and that commanded a substantial measure of international respect. Yet despite the tenacity with which Hughes pressed his views on this matter, he was unsuccessful. In April, before the American Society of International Law, and in June, speaking at Columbia and at Dartmouth, he tried to clarify the question and to answer the objections that had already been raised. But the Court was, in a sense, a creation of the League. And the League was anathema to the Republican irreconcilables. Nothing whatsoever had been accomplished when the Secretary laid down his charge on March 4, 1925.

In other matters, however, involving cooperation with Geneva, and not requiring Senate action, Hughes edged forward during his term of office. He sent no representative to the Conference on Communication and Transit held at Barcelona in 1921, but to do so he would have had to reverse the decision of his predecessor. He declined to ratify the Treaty of Saint-Germain, which regulated the arms traffic, and which was tied up with the League;

to have acted otherwise would have involved troublesome discussion with the Senate. But in 1923 American representatives took part in deliberations of the Council in which a loan for the settlement of Greek refugees was discussed. In that same year an American delegation sat with a committee of the Assembly which was engaged in drafting a convention to deal with the international traffic in opium, and participated in a conference on the same subject in 1924. American observers had a hand in other discussions on such questions as the white-slave traffic and the suppression of obscene publications. Insignificant as these matters were, they led the way to more important forms of association, such as participation in the Preparatory Commission on Disarmament in the next administration. And they illustrated perfectly the principle on which Hughes desired to act — conference, yes; commitment, no.

In reviewing the entire record with regard to the League, it is highly important to place the question in a proper historical perspective. Hughes never believed that failure to join the world organization had much to do with the chapters of tragedy written in the 1930s, with the aggressions of Mussolini and of Hitler. He called attention to the failure of France and Great Britain to fulfill their own League engagements to the full in this period. He never felt that the story would have been different if in 1921 the United States had put its full authority behind the principle of collective security. His position is plausible, though not necessarily convincing. While the question is purely hypothetical, one thing can be said with certainty. As a practical matter the American people were by no means prepared at that time to assume the sweeping responsibilities that were involved in the Wilsonian formula. Hughes acted, in the last analysis, within the framework of American public opinion.

In summing up Hughes's point of view on the larger aspects of the League, it seems fair to say that he was, while not always free from party spirit, never steeped in that partisan venom which was again and again demonstrated by some of the Republican Senators in connection with the treaty battle. His position was dignified and worthy of respect. If there is a criticism to be made, it is that what was involved in the struggle over the League was much more than legal formulae. Hughes's animadversions on the Covenant, even if one regards them as incontrovertible, reflected the reaction towards nationalism that followed hard on the war. Had the Covenant been accepted as it stood, its defects and its exaggerated hopes might have been cured by interpretation and its usefulness much increased by the adhesion of the United States. Whether the issue called for caution or for optimism and faith is a question which will long be debated, and which most persons will no doubt answer in accord with their temperaments and their memories.

V

Secretary of State

The Washington Conference and the Reparations Problem

HUGHES BECAME SECRETARY OF STATE on March 4, 1921. For the next four years he was wholly engrossed in the problems of his office. He was left an unusually free hand by President Harding, who, indeed, was little qualified to lead in foreign affairs. In return, except for an occasional political speech, he virtually never intervened in the broader political field. He knew nothing of the scandals that were to rock the country after the death of the President. The unsavory deals with regard to the oil reserves of Elk Hills and Teapot Dome were never brought before the Cabinet. His only connection with them was in urging a housecleaning after they had been revealed. True, he was ready to defend the Republican Party in 1924 and to maintain, somewhat sophistically, that guilt was personal and constituted no indictment of the party organization. But he can be exculpated completely from any knowledge of the irregularities, and he urged the punishment of the offenders. The explanation of his limited interest in these matters lies in his complete devotion to his office, and in his conviction that his chief, if not his sole, responsibility was to serve the country as Secretary of State.

In his work as Secretary of State, Hughes showed, as always, a profound instinct for effective administration. The diplomatic service of the United States had too often been the sport of politics. The Rogers Act of 1924 was in no small measure due to the Secretary's inspiration. By this fundamental piece of legislation, salaries, heretofore egregiously low, were raised; the diplomatic and consular services were merged, with transfer from one to the other made possible; appointments and promotions were based on merit; and a pension system was instituted. In the opinion of a highly competent judge, this enactment produced a "vastly superior organization" to that which had existed before.

Hughes came into office at a time when the tide of nationalism was running high. He had to contend against a strong current of isolationism at home, against mounting resentment at the United States abroad, and against serious problems in the Orient. When one considers the difficulties he faced, his record was remarkable. The thorniest question that confronted him when he took office was the tension which existed between the United States and Japan, and the related question of naval rivalry with Japan and Great Britain.

The period of the First World War, like the period of the Second, seemed to the Japanese a golden opportunity.

They promptly declared war on Germany (in August 1914) and soon reduced the German stronghold of Kiaochou on the coast of China in the province of Shantung. They picked up the German islands in the Pacific in concert with the British. In 1915 they presented to the weak government of the Chinese Republic the twenty-one demands which, in their original form, looked to nothing less than a Japanese protectorate. Though these demands were eventually reduced, they nonetheless marked a stage in the Japanese advance in the Orient. Finally in 1918 came the intervention in Siberia. This intervention was undertaken in concert with the United States, or perhaps it would be better to say that President Wilson had acquiesced in American cooperation as a means of watching the Japanese. But the forces of Nippon were still there after the Americans had withdrawn, one of many grounds for distrust of the government of Tokyo.

The situation was aggravated by the naval rivalry that had sprung up during the war and that involved Great Britain as well as Japan. Though President Wilson never took a rough attitude towards British violation of neutral rights at sea, such as might have stirred up the American public, many Americans resented the overlordship of Britain. When the preparedness movement began to sweep the country, it stimulated interest in the development of naval strength; and the Chief Executive associated himself with this feeling when he declared that the United States should have incomparably the most adequate navy in the world. The demand for parity with Britain became a kind of cliché before the end of the war. At the same time Japan took very seriously the American building program, and launched a formidable program of her own. The stage was set for what might have been a serious three-sided naval competition, a competition exacerbated in the case of Nippon by the political factors already mentioned.

Furthermore, an Anglo-Japanese alliance troubled American opinion. The British and Japanese governments were bound by a treaty which might conceivably be directed against the United States. True, when this alliance had been renewed in 1911, the British had made an effort to quiet American fears by inserting in the treaty a provision that it should not apply against any nation with which Britain had a treaty of arbitration, and then by negotiating such a treaty with this country. But the arbitration treaty ran afoul of the normal difficulties for such instruments in the Senate of the United States, and on its failure the situation remained clouded. There was a touchy problem here when the new Secretary of State took office.

There was every reason, moreover, why a resolute effort should be made to deal with it. There was great congressional pressure for the reduction of armaments, reflected in the passage in the Senate, in May of 1921, of a resolution introduced by Senator Borah calling upon the President to initiate a conference on the subject. There was also the political necessity of meeting in some way the demands of the peace lovers who might take ill the cold attitude of the administration towards the League. In a sense the Washington conference was a Republican something-just-as-good-or-better to meet the rejected prescription of the Democrats for international concord. By the early summer of 1921, it was clear that some kind of positive action was demanded by the exigencies of the matter.

Yet it was the British who took the initiative. As so often in diplomatic history they had a keen weather eye to good relations with the United States. They did not propose to jeopardize those relations. As early as March 16, 1921, Lord Lee of Fareham, the First Lord of the Admiralty, had already admitted the principle of parity in Anglo-American relations. In April, through Adolph Ochs, the publisher of the *New York Times,* he signified unofficially his willingness to begin negotiations with the United States. This gesture strengthened the hands of the administration.

In June another event took place which brought a new encouragement to Washington. The British Imperial Conference convened in London. There the Canadian prime minister, Mr. Meighen (this was the period of brief interruption of the thirty years' rule of MacKenzie King), stoutly argued against the pending renewal of the Anglo-Japanese alliance. He brought the conference to accept the idea of a more generalized understanding, in which Great Britain, the United States, Japan, and China should all take part. His victory pointed straight towards the idea of an international conference in which naval and Far Eastern questions should both be considered.

On July 5, Lord Curzon, the British prime minister, proposed to the American ambassador that the President convene such a conference. But the American Secretary of State was anxious to make it appear that the initiative came from the United States, and the British were ready to agree. The first news that the outside world had of the projected conference was a press release by President Harding on July 11 in which it was announced that the Washington government was inviting the interested powers to a conference on the reduction of armaments and on the situation in the Far East. The initiative which Hughes thus seized at the very outset was in many respects to be his throughout the negotiations that followed. On the question of the Anglo-Japanese alliance and on the questions of the Far East the meeting at Washington was in many, though not in all, respects one in which the American view prevailed.

The most dramatic aspect of the conference by all odds was the agreement with regard to naval ratios. In preparation for the diplomatic battle Hughes adopted at the outset a fundamental principle, namely, that the only way to arrive at agreement was to fix naval power on the basis of existing strength. Elaborate tables were prepared in collaboration with the navy as to the number of capital ships each nation possessed, taking into account not only vessels completed and commissioned, but vessels under construction. With these tables as a guide the Secretary worked out what came to be known as the 5-5-3 formula, giving to the United States, Great Britain, and Japan battleships in these proportions. In order to carry out this formula, all three great naval nations would have to scrap a part of their existing tonnage in vessels built or building; since Great Britain would have to make the greatest sacrifices in vessels actually launched and in service, some concession was made to her at the outset; but after an interval of years, allowing for obsolescence and rebuilding, the proposed ratio would be in virtually full effect. In the course of this process the United States would have abandoned its 1916 naval program and in vessels built *and building* have made the greatest sacrifices of any one of the three powers.

Hughes arrived at this method of naval reduction only after meeting sharp opposition at home. The General Board of the Navy at the outset believed that the United States should have a navy as large as that of Great Britain and Japan combined; nor after it had given ground on this point was it in enthusiastic accord with the Secretary of State with regard to a program which called for the curtailment of a program which it had recommended only a few years before. Hughes's ability to impose his point of view (albeit with some assistance in the Navy Department and with the loyal cooperation of the Assistant Secretary, Theodore Roosevelt, Jr.) is an extraordinary example of the subordination of the military to the civil power. It is impossible not to admit the courage, tenacity, and rationality of the Secretary of State.

Even more significant was the way in which the new naval formula was handled in the conference itself. The conference opened on November 12. The day before the body of the Unknown Soldier had been carried to its last resting place in Arlington amidst moving demonstrations of the desire of the American people for peace. A more propitious moment could hardly have been chosen for Hughes's maneuver. What he did was nonetheless unprecedented. Beginning his opening speech to the great assemblage with the customary generalities, he went on to publish to the world the actual plan for naval reduction and to confront the astonished delegates with a scheme not only for the diminution of the American navy but for the diminution of the Japanese and British navies as well. There has perhaps never been a diplomatic episode quite like that of November 12. The Secretary's proposal produced an almost indescribable enthusiasm. A "tornado of cheering" burst forth. As one trained journalist described the scene, "Hats waved, handkerchiefs fluttered, men shook one another's hands, hugged one another, slapped one another, exhibited every kind of animal delight of which human beings are capable in their high moments." And the exaltation of that moment was communicated through the press to large numbers of Americans throughout the land.

Of course the Secretary's gesture was not the beginning of that open diplomacy which has played such a large part in American history. More than any other people the Americans have debated their foreign affairs in an open forum, in Congress, and in presidential messages, and in the public prints. President Wilson, going further than any of his predecessors, had published contemporaneously with the event his important dispatches to foreign governments, and had used the weapon of open diplomacy well in the period of the war. But the striking thing about the Hughes proposal is its extraordinarily concrete character, its precision. Imaginative in its conception, it was practical in its content. None but a statesman of high talents (one almost says of genius) could have conceived and executed this tour de force.

It was, of course, one thing to propose and another to carry through to completion. In the main in the negotiations that followed the British accepted the American formula. The principal difficulties in the negotiations came, as might have been expected, from Japan. The Japanese people had long been indoctrinated with the idea of a 10-7 rather than a 10-6 ratio. Moreover, the program set forth in the Secretary's opening speech called for the scrapping of the battleship *Mutsu,* which had a special sentimental value for the Japanese, and the destruction of which the Japanese delegation bitterly resisted. Their insistence on this point led to a revision of the arrangements, which dramatically illustrated the cooperative position of the British in the conference. The *Mutsu,* it was agreed, would be kept. But this compelled the British to build two new superdreadnoughts, so the British naval leaders insisted, and these vessels were to be of a tonnage of 49,000 tons, far more than any ships in existence. Such a proposal seemed to Hughes completely inacceptable. He did not see how a conference on reduction of armaments could possibly sanction a proposal that called for ships greater than any ever built. In a private meeting on December 15 he strongly urged his view on Mr. Balfour, the British Foreign Secretary. And Balfour did what, in a sense, Hughes himself had earlier done. He overruled his naval advisers and agreed that the two new ships to be built should not exceed 37,000 tons.

There was another difficulty alongside that created by

Japanese insistence on the *Mutsu*. The Japanese could not consent to the 5-5-3 ratio unless some kind of nonfortification agreement were made with regard to the Pacific islands. Originally they proposed that the United States should consent not to increase its fortifications in Guam, the Philippines, or Hawaii in return for a similar agreement on their part with regard to Formosa, the Pescadores, and Oshima. As to Hawaii the Secretary would make no concession, but after a good deal of discussion a satisfactory formula was worked out with regard to the other two American-held islands, and the way was thus cleared for an accord on the naval ratios.

There can be little doubt that in entering into this agreement Hughes acted wisely despite the opposition of the naval authorities. He faced a practical situation. In no case would Congress have voted funds for building up American power in Guam or the Philippines. It hesitated to do so in a much more threatening situation in the 1930s. Even Senator Lodge, the friend of a large navy and a confirmed nationalist in his policies, agreed that there was no hope whatsoever of persuading his congressional colleagues to alter their point of view. On paper Hughes gave up a great deal and presented Japan with a position of extraordinary security against immediate attack in the Orient. But from a more realistic point of view he gave up nothing at all. His sensitiveness to criticism on this point in later years is understandable; the judgment of history weighs heavily in his favor. It is significant that the naval treaty was ratified with only one dissenting vote in the Senate of the United States.

A third roadblock in the way of completing the treaty for reduction of armaments was created by France. The French came to Washington in a distinctly touchy frame of mind, as was well illustrated by Premier Briand's annoyance at the opening meeting of the conference when he was placed around the corner of the table from the other chief delegates, denied, as he claimed, the *"place d'honneur."* The French were not overjoyed at the fact that the naval negotiations were carried on by the three great naval powers and that they were, at the first, excluded. In choosing the most expeditious course Hughes had wounded their *amour-propre.*

Accordingly, when the agreement of the big three was imminent, France came forward with a demand for a naval force of 350,000 tons, which bore no relationship to the Hughes formula. There was acid discussion between the Secretary and Sarrault, the French naval minister and, after Briand's return to Paris, the head of the French delegation. Hughes was getting nowhere. Reluctantly, he decided to appeal by cable directly to the premier and, after consultation with Jusserand, the French ambassador, did so. He proposed for France the very generous figure of 175,000 tons, far more than the principle of the ratios would have permitted. And he got back from Briand the necessary positive assurance. But there was a fly in the ointment, even so. There had been some hope of extending the agreement with regard to battleships to other categories, and Hughes had proposed this in his opening speech. The French position made that impossible. The only abovewater craft whose numbers were limited at

Washington were battleships and aircraft carriers. It was France, too, but with much more reason, that from the beginning of the conference prevented any serious discussion of land armaments. Not unnaturally, the French connected any discussion of this question with assurances as to their own security, particularly from Great Britain and the United States. It was quite impossible to give such assurances. So this whole matter was relegated to the background.

Closely related to the problem of armament was that of the Anglo-Japanese alliance. As we have already seen, this alliance was a subject of concern to the United States. It is obvious, also, that British statesmanship, however attached to the connection with Nippon, had as a primary objective good relations with the United States. At the outset of the conference Mr. Balfour attempted to reconcile conflicting British interests by virtually proposing a three-power alliance instead of a dual one. Obviously, this would never do. Such a proposal would not only get short shrift in the Senate, but it would commit the United States in some measure to the defense of Japanese imperialism on the Asiatic mainland. In negotiations which were largely personal, and the full content of which has never been revealed, Hughes proposed a wholly different plan. He suggested a four-power treaty between the United States, Great Britain, France, and Japan which should bind the signatories, first, to consult together in case of any dispute arising with regard to "their insular dominions and possessions in the region of the Pacific Ocean," and, second, to communicate with each other "fully and frankly as to the most efficient measures to be taken, jointly or separately, to meet the exigencies" of a situation created by a threat to their rights from some other power.

This proposal is interesting from several points of view. In the first place, by the inclusion of France as the fourth power something was done to assuage the wounded pride of that state, and at a time when relations were particularly strained. It is even possible that Hughes's proposal, made on December 11, had something to do with Briand's acquiescence on the question of battleship tonnage a few days later.

In the second place, the proposal provided in specific terms for the termination of the Anglo-Japanese alliance. At the same time the provisions with regard to aggression by an outside power at least adumbrated the possibility of joint action by Great Britain and Japan against the Soviet Union, or even against an aggressive China. In the third place, the treaty guaranteed the safety of the Philippines from attack — at least as far as words could do this. In the fourth place, the language limiting the operation of the treaty to the islands of the Pacific left open for future discussion the problem of China. And finally, as originally drafted, it provided a kind of guarantee of Japan, since it was understood on all sides that the Japanese main islands were themselves included. Looking at it as a whole, one can see that it certainly advanced American interests, and at the price of no painful concession.

Nonetheless, it faced rough going before it was ratified. The treaty was finally assented to, 67 to 27. A change of five votes would have defeated it. A tempest was stirred up when President Harding, imperfectly informed, declared at a press conference that in his judgment it did not apply to the Japanese mainland. Superheated patriots saw in a possible guarantee of Nippon something highly dangerous. This difficulty was overcome by a supplementary agreement specifically limiting the treaty, so far as Japan was concerned, to her island possessions. But in the Senate the compact came in for sharp attack upon the part of the irreconcilables. After much friction it was finally accepted with only the reservation — the superfluous reservation — that it involved "no commitment to armed force, no alliance, no obligation to join in any defense." In connection with its ratification Hughes wrote a letter which has a more than historical significance. "I am at a loss to understand," he declared, "how those who have attained the high position of Senator can permit themselves to indulge in reckless characterization of other peoples and to manifest in a manner so injurious to the conduct of our foreign relations their opposition to the work of the conference. There is certainly cause for anxiety when the results of the most earnest endeavor under American auspices come so near to defeat at the hands of the Senate."

The Washington Conference also devoted some of its deliberations to China. In November of 1921, there were grave apprehensions as to the future of that troubled country. American sentiment had been formed long before, and inevitably constituted the basis on which the Secretary of State was obliged to act. That sentiment, expressed in the

Open Door notes of John Hay more than twenty years before, called for the preservation of the territorial integrity of the Chinese state and for equality of opportunity in the field of commerce and concessions. These excellent principles had frequently been violated in practice, and flagrantly challenged in the Twenty-one Demands. What could be done with regard to this problem?

With regard to the policy of the Open Door, Hughes took the lead in negotiating what was later to be known as the Nine-Power Treaty. For the first time in our history, and where Hay had failed, he secured formal treaty recognition of the principles by which the United States wished all the powers in the Orient to be guided. The powers pledged themselves to respect the sovereignty and independence of China, to give China the "fullest and most unembarrassed opportunity to maintain a stable government, to use their influence for the purpose of effectually maintaining the principle of equal opportunity for the commerce and industry of all nations throughout the territory, and to refrain from taking advantage of conditions in China in order to seek special rights and privileges which would abridge the rights of citizens of friendly states, and from countenancing action inimical to the security of such states."

But beyond that Hughes was not able to go. He sought, for example, to secure an examination of existing commitments and concessions in China, and to set up machinery to test their validity. He was defeated. He proposed the creation of a board of reference to which disputed questions for the future might be submitted. Again he failed. He sought to strengthen the position of China by giving her fuller control of her customs administration, and by permitting her to levy higher duties than those which had been imposed upon her by unequal treaties with other states. He made only a minimum of progress. In no substantial way did he shake the favored position which the Japanese enjoyed in Manchuria.

He was a little more successful with regard to Shantung. As we have already said, some measure of success on this matter was vital. The Chinese came to Washington prepared to insist on the unequivocal surrender of Japan to their demands. They were persuaded, with difficulty, to enter into conversations with the Japanese delegates. They were hampered at home by the crude nationalistic sentiment to be expected from young and relatively weak nations faced with powerful neighbors. It was therefore something of a success for Hughes to bring them to the conference table at all, a success only accomplished by much urging and by threats of the forfeiture of world opinion, and finally sealed by a highly opportune change of regime at Peiping.

But to some extent the final settlement gave Japan the substance, and China the shadow. The Chinese were to buy back the railway line which gave economic control of the province, but only over a term of years. And during this period China was to employ a Japanese traffic manager and a Japanese chief accountant. In addition the treaty was so drawn as to give to the government in Tokyo means of prolonging its control.

On one final question the American Secretary of State secured a concession that may or may not have been a matter of substance. When the conference met in the fall of 1921, Japanese troops, as we have mentioned, remained in Siberia. Though the United States had not recognized the Soviet regime, it still made itself the guardian of the integrity of Russian territory. And in accord with this principle, Hughes urged upon the Japanese some assurance as to their future intentions. The assurance was given, but without limit of time. It still remains a moot question whether the Secretary in this regard secured a genuine victory or whether the subsequent action of the Japanese Government in honoring this pledge was induced as much by disgust with the whole adventure as by pressure from the United States.

Few diplomatic conferences met with more acclaim at the time than that of Washington. The fact is incontestable that it relaxed the international tensions of the postwar era, that it opened the way to wide economies in naval building, that it dissolved the Anglo-Japanese alliance (so great a source of concern to the United States), and that it gave formal recognition to the American point of view with regard to China. Viewed in the light of the time, it deserved to be hailed as a great achievement.

But in the changing events of the 1940s it came in for very severe criticism. Hughes was accused of sacrificing the essential interests of the United States. A partisan critic asserted in 1944 that he had sunk more of our fleet than the Japanese did at Pearl Harbor. The concessions that he had made in the nonfortification agreement were denounced as adding to the costs and burdens of the war which broke out in 1941.

In any specific sense, such criticisms are absurd and unjust. As we have already stated, there was not the slightest chance of Congress appropriating funds for building up our strength in Guam and in the Philippines. Congress, indeed, not only declined to accept this responsibility but, in the years following, under both Democratic and Republican control, even went so far as to fail to keep the navy up to the standard fixed at Washington. Essentially and fundamentally, the Hughes policies were based upon American reluctance to face the facts of power insofar as the Orient was concerned.

This reluctance is the heart of the matter. The Washington treaties *did* leave the United States in an unfavorable position from which to apply physical force. But the Secretary acted in the frame of reference of his time. All statesmanship in a democracy is and must be in its broad lines interpretative of the national sentiment. It is idle, to use one of the Secretary's favorite phrases, to quarrel with a political leader for acting within the limits imposed upon him by the state of the public mind.

But one can go further. The Washington arms treaty, from one angle of vision, was a great experiment. It could be defended at the time on the ground that it gave Japan security in the Far East, and that to give such security was to strengthen the Japanese moderates and to stimulate, if not to ensure, the domination of these elements. It was, in this sense, a "noble experiment." And for a time it may be said to have worked. The less aggressive elements in Japan remained in power for almost a decade after the solemn signing of the treaties of Washington.

In the long run, however, it did *not* work. The structure that Hughes had done so much to erect in Washington lay in ruins by 1935. The forces of Japanese militarism and aggression were only temporarily restrained. They were by no means exorcised. In retrospect the story has its moral. The American people, with their preoccupation with material interest and with their undoubted idealism, have liked to believe that good will was a solvent in the field of international relations. They have accepted with reluctance in the international sphere the fundamental truth — and it is a fundamental truth — that power is of the very essence of international politics. Not abdication but the restrained use of physical force seems to be the wise policy in such matters. Just as the mass of Americans could not see that the principle of collective security in some form, perhaps an attenuated form, was the necessary condition of European stability after 1919, so they could not see in 1921 that to get out of the Orient physically, while continuing to cherish mental, moral, and economic prepossessions with regard to it, was in the long run unlikely to prove sound policy.

The criticism just made with regard to the naval treaties applies to the Nine-Power Pact as well. It may be conceded this this pact strengthened the moral position of the United States. But since it contained no machinery for enforcement, it turned out in the long run to be ineffectual. The vast changes that were taking place in the Orient were not fundamentally affected by the words written on parchment at Washington in 1922. One may go further, perhaps. The idea of a strong China, open on equal terms to the capital and commerce of the world, an idea deeply cherished in the United States, has turned out to be an illusion. Here again it was in 1921-1922, and it is today, difficult for vast numbers of our people to face the realities of the international situation. We were not ready to *enforce* our view of things in China. We were only ready to engage in moral homilies and, from time to time and in limited ways, to show our sympathy with what we fondly — and romantically — hoped would be the development of a democratic state. But the great issues of the East, like those to which a great German statesman had alluded in another epoch, were to be settled by blood and iron. The American people recoiled against any such conclusion. They were not prepared then (have they ever been prepared?) to apply in the Orient the amount of physical force which would, conceivably, permit them to carry out their own ideas. The Nine-Power Treaty was a classical example of the exaggerated American faith in paper promises, and of our frequent failure as a people to look the hard facts of life in the face.

For the time being, however, the high hopes raised by the Washington treaties seemed possible of realization. In the main, in the decade of the 1920s, it was possible to view the course of events in China with hope and to rejoice in the comparative relaxation of our relations with

Japan. Only one incident in the course of Hughes's incumbency at the State Department seriously marred this happy picture, and this was one in which he strove in vain to moderate the forces of demagogy that are always latent, and sometimes active, in American life. This incident was the controversy over the immigration bill in 1924.

The end of the First World War had seen, as one of the many evidences of the nationalistic spirit, the growth of the movement for immigration restriction. This movement took form in legislation creating the quota system, restricting the number of immigrants from each nation to a fixed proportion of those of the same nationality already in the country.

But this rule had never been applied to Japan. On the contrary, immigration from Nippon had been regulated by the "gentlemen's agreement" which severely limited access to the United States and which in a period of fifteen years resulted in the admission of only 8681 Japanese. It was this agreement which was jeopardized by the legislation introduced in Congress in December 1923 which excluded all aliens ineligible to citizenship — a backhanded way of describing the Japanese under existing statutes.

There were strong arguments against such legislation. There existed no danger of a flood of immigrants from Japan. The gentlemen's agreement had been working well, as the figures cited attested. Furthermore, if Congress were to apply the quota system to Japan, the result would be a mere trickle of immigration and the Japanese would be placed upon a precisely similar footing with other races. Considerations of prudence, of comity, of wisdom suggested that the problem be attacked from some other angle than that of the bill put forward in the House.

Hughes saw this clearly. When the Japanese ambassador, Mr. Hanihara, voiced his apprehensions with regard to the measure, the Secretary immediately wrote to the chairman of the House committee in charge of the legislation. "The Japanese are a sensitive people," he wrote, "and unquestionably would regard such a legislative enactment as fixing a stigma upon them. I regret to be compelled to say that I believe such legislative action would largely undo the work of the Washington Conference on Limitation of Armaments, which so greatly improved our relations with Japan. The question is presented whether it is worth while thus to affront a friendly nation with whom we have established the most cordial relations, and what gain would there be from such action?"

At the same time the Secretary was aware of the difficulties involved in the situation from the point of view of the exclusionists. The gentlemen's agreement was, after all, informal; it rested upon correspondence which could only be seen with the permission of Japan; and, at the time, its actual operation was obscure. Hughes therefore suggested to Mr. Hanihara, the Japanese ambassador, that he write the State Department setting forth the essential facts from the point of view of the Japanese Government. This Hanihara did in a letter which, had it been received in good spirit, ought to have set many doubts to rest.

But in this letter occurred a hornet of a paragraph, as

was soon to be shown. "Relying upon the confidence you have been good enough to show me at all times," it declared, "I have stated or rather repeated all this to you very candidly and in a most friendly spirit, for I realize, as I believe you do, the grave consequences which the enactment of the measure retaining that particular provision would inevitably bring upon the otherwise happy and mutually advantageous relations between our two countries."

The Hanihara note was read by the Secretary before its transmission to Congress. He noted the phrase "grave consequences" and was conscious of its infelicity. He might perhaps have suggested to Hanihara that it be modified. But the matter seemed to him a small one in view of the conciliatory tone of the communication taken as a whole. He also wished to act promptly in view of the fact that the House bill was then being debated. He therefore sent the letter on to Capitol Hill. Greatly to his surprise, there followed a flare-up of substantial proportions. Two days later the House passed the immigration bill with the offending clause included by the substantial vote of 323 to 71. In the Senate a heated debate ensued. Senator Henry Cabot Lodge, apparently heedless of his obligation as chairman of the Foreign Relations Committee to support the administration, denounced the language of the Japanese ambassador as a "veiled threat" to the United States. An amendment to recognize the gentlemen's agreement was defeated by the crashing vote of 76 to 2. The bill itself passed by an overwhelming majority. A last effort of the administration, while the bill was in conference, to secure postponement of the exclusion clause for a period of two years met with utter failure. So strong was the feeling that it seemed useless to suggest to President Coolidge that he veto the measure.

It is understandable that the action of Congress created profound resentment in Japan. "It seems safe to say," says one of the ablest commentators on the subject, "that the American people have never resented any policy pursued by Japan in China or elsewhere as deeply, as unanimously and with as poignant a sense of injustice, as the Japanese have resented the statutory exclusion of 1924." Inevitably the Japanese ambassador was compelled to present a dignified protest, and just as inevitably Hughes found himself in the position of being compelled to defend the action of Congress as an exercise of the sovereign right of controlling immigration on the part of the United States. Somewhat lamely he concluded his answering note with these words: "I desire once more to emphasize the appreciation on the part of this Government of the voluntary cooperation of your Government in carrying out the gentlemen's agreement and to express the conviction that the right of each Government to legislate in control of immigration should not derogate in any degree from the mutual good will and cordial friendship which have always characterized the relations of the two countries."

In a letter to a friend of his Hughes expressed something of his disgust at the whole episode. "It is a sorry business," he wrote, "and I am greatly depressed. It has undone the work of the Washington Conference and implanted the seeds of an antagonism which are sure to bear fruit in the future. . . . The question is not one of war but of the substitution of antagonism for cooperation in the Far East, with all that that involves. Our friends in the Senate have in a few minutes spoiled the work of years and done a lasting injury to our common country." The judgment may have been oversevere, but no student of the period can doubt the deep sincerity behind the Secretary's words or fail to deplore the manner in which the national legislature on this occasion, as on some occasions before or since, dealt an unnecessary blow to the effective development of the foreign policy of the United States.

Reparations and War Debts

The immigration debate of 1924 revealed how deep-seated was the virus of nationalism in the United States and with what ease appeal could be made to the spirit of xenophobia. In another area of the world the same disease was raging. France, in the years after the war, suffered from a deep-seated complex of fear and hate with regard to Germany. And this fear and hate made extraordinarily difficult the settlement of the vexed question of reparations.

Woodrow Wilson had hoped that this question might be settled by a Reparations Commission in which the American representative, as chairman, would have the deciding voice. But the Senate not only defeated the Treaty of Versailles but in the separate peace with Germany, negotiated by Hughes in 1921, tacked on a reservation by which such representation, or indeed representation on any of the numerous bodies functioning under the pact, was forbidden without the explicit consent of Congress. Hughes was thus hamstrung in dealing with a matter of momentous import, with a problem that culminated in the French invasion of the Ruhr, in the catastrophic currency inflation in Germany, and (some persons would argue) in that partial destruction in Germany of the middle classes which prepared the way for Adolf Hitler. One asks oneself whether the Secretary, on this specific question, made as vigorous a stand as he might have. But one remembers, too, that he was dealing with other matters of vast import on which the support of the legislators was essential.

In any case, there was nothing for Hughes to do in the circumstances but to let the reparations question simmer. He was well advised in declining to mediate between the Germans and the claimant powers in the spring of 1921, but he did offer to transmit to the Allies any proposal which the government of the Reich might care to make. The offer was accepted; a proposition of much merit was formulated in Berlin and sent forward by the Secretary with the suggestion that it might form a basis of discussion. But the French still had extravagant dreams of what might be extorted from the Reich, and the proposition was rejected. By a virtual ultimatum, Germany was compelled to accept a reparations burden which was bound to cause trouble in the future and which made impossible the reasonable solution of the whole problem, the floating of a great international loan by the Reich.

In 1921 and 1922 the attitude of France became

stiffer and stiffer. The situation was shaping up towards sanctions and military pressure on Germany. Such a development Hughes profoundly deplored. The elementary unwisdom of attempting to collect vast sums by force he pointed out again and again to the harassed French ambassador at Washington, M. Jusserand. As early as September, 1922, he proposed that the question be taken out of politics by submitting it to a group of financial experts. And in December, in a new stroke of public diplomacy (which he later told his biographer came from God), he brought this whole idea forward in a speech made before the American Historical Association at New Haven. "Why should they [the Allies]," he asked, "not invite men of the highest authority in finance in their respective countries — men of such prestige, experience and honor that their agreement upon the amount to be paid [by Germany], and upon a financial plan for working out the payments, would be accepted throughout the world as the most authoritative expression obtainable?" And he added, "I have no doubt that distinguished Americans would be willing to serve on such a commission."

In this last sentence was the essence of the matter. Since the American members of the investigatory body would be appointed by the Reparations Commission itself, there could be no interference from Congress. Hughes had thus planned to outflank the Senate.

At the time it was pronounced, the New Haven speech had no practical effect whatsoever. Early in the next year, over British opposition, the Reparations Commission, presided over by a French chairman, declared Germany in default. Not many days later, the French moved into the Ruhr.

The months that followed amply attested the folly of the French experiment. The Germans retaliated by passive resistance. The situation went from bad to worse. Hughes waited patiently (or perhaps not so patiently) for the lesson of experience to take hold. On November 23, 1923, after many months, the Reparations Commission approved an inquiry of the type that the Secretary had suggested, and two committees of experts were appointed to consider the whole problem. On these commissions Americans were represented.

The result was what came to be known as the Dawes plan. This plan was no final solution of an intricate problem. It left the total amount of reparations payments still in doubt and, as a necessary corollary, the term over which payments should be made. But it provided for a schedule of payments, for an international loan to Germany, and for the stabilization of her currency, and immensely eased the tension that had been created. It paved the way, also, for a political understanding between France and Germany which, at the time, appeared to open up a great vista of hope for the future.

Hughes himself played an important part in what went forward. Ostensibly going to Europe as president of the American Bar Association (a camouflage that seems a bit ineffective, if not comic), he visited the various capitals and lent his influence to persuading the governments concerned to accept the Dawes program. He appears to have had his greatest difficulties in France, where Premier Herriot, himself not unfavorable to the plan, was afraid of the hostile influence of Raymond Poincaré. But he saw both Herriot and Poincaré and talked to them in no uncertain terms. "If you turn this down, America is through," he told his biographer he said to the former premier. Just how decisive his role was, it is impossible to say. But at any rate the plan was adopted and helped immensely to give Europe a few years of tranquillity.

Closely allied with the question of reparations was the question of war debts. As we have already seen, the settlement of this matter was hampered by the very strong public opinion in the United States which demanded repayment in full of the more than ten billions of dollars advanced by the American Government to its associates. In the wave of postwar nationalism most Americans saw only that they had come to the rescue of the Western democracies in a great war, that they had played a decisive part in the winning of that war, and that the United States had little to show in the way of material gain for the immense sums of money that had been expended and for the loss of American lives. The suggestion that they should now forgive borrowings which had been understood to be such at the time they were made was hardly to be tolerated. Hughes therefore operated within very narrow limits in dealing with this important question.

He was hampered, too, by the determination of the Congress to retain control of the whole matter. In February of 1922 the national legislature created a special war-debts commission, composed of the Secretary of State, the Secretary of the Treasury, and members of both Houses. The original act confined the commission narrowly with regard to the terms on which refunding could take place. No new bonds were to be issued the date of maturity of which was later than June 15, 1947, and the rate of interest was not to be fixed at less than 4¼ per cent.

The legislation of 1922 produced no great enthusiasm in Europe, and it was indeed fundamentally vulnerable. For as the rate of interest fell in the United States and the American Government could borrow at a rate substantially lower than that of the war years, it seemed unreasonable to exact a high rate from other governments. It was also apparent that, if interest were to be added to principal, there was little chance of arriving at agreements which stipulated for the complete discharge of the debt by 1947.

The Congress was therefore obliged to enact a much more flexible statute in the winter of 1923. It was undoubtedly influenced by the negotiations with Great Britain which took place in January of that year. In the discussions which followed, Secretary Mellon, the chairman of the commission, took a leading part, but Hughes was, of course, associated with him. He was much annoyed by the part played by Ambassador Harvey, the political appointee of the administration as ambassador to London, who gave to the British wholly unauthorized assurances as to the rate of interest and as to the possibility of floating a tax-free loan in the United States. But in due course an arrangement was arrived at, the rate of interest reduced, the period of payment extended to sixty-two years, and this agreement was approved by the Congress. Though the agreements with France and Italy were not consummated until the next administration, and then on much more generous terms, at least the initial steps were taken in the period of Hughes's service at the State Department.

What seems remarkable, in the context of our own time, is that, so far as we can tell from the record, Hughes never saw the contradiction between the debt-refunding policies and the tariff policy of the administration. To demand repayment on a large scale and then to raise higher than ever before the barriers against imports was a policy that could hardly be justified. But there is no indication that this fact was ever emphasized by the Secretary of State in dealing with the problem. The enactment of the Fordney-McCumber bill in 1922 met with no objection whatsoever so far as Hughes was concerned. In this, as in other matters, he was no doubt influenced and confined by the nationalistic temper of the time.

Problems of Recognition

There is one other aspect of our foreign policy with regard to Europe that we must discuss before turning our attention to Latin America. That is the question of Russia. The central question was whether the United States should recognize the Communist regime set up by the revolution of November 1917. There were those who would have answered this question in the affirmative, notably the leader of the irreconcilables in the Senate, William E. Borah of Idaho. The government of Lenin, so the argument ran, was firmly established in power. The traditional policy of the United States was oriented towards the recognition of *de facto* regimes, as indicated in the famous message of President Monroe. The resumption of diplomatic relations with Moscow, it was further argued, would encourage trade between the two countries and promote the commercial interests of the United States.

But Hughes could not and did not accept this view. In repudiating it he was but following the example set by the preceding administration and endorsed by the two that followed. The course of his argument was brilliantly stated in his response to a Women's Committee for Recognition of Russia in March of 1923. Hughes pointed out, correctly, that there was little to be gained economically by establishing closer relations with the Kremlin. Investment in a Communist country was hazardous if not impossible. There was nothing, he said, to show that the countries which had acknowledged the Bolshevik regime fared better with regard to trade than those which had declined or hesitated to do so. But, in Hughes's view, the case ran deeper. Before this it had sometimes been made a condition of recognition that a country should fulfill its international obligations. There was no indication whatsoever that the Kremlin intended to recognize the debts of its predecessors; it had, indeed, annulled them. There was no indication that it was ready to offer compensation for the confiscation of American property in Russia; in fact, quite the contrary. Concessions America might make; but the principle involved in acknowledgment of just obligations was another matter. In addition, the Secretary called the attention of his hearers to the fact that the Communist regime encouraged world revolution, that it could hardly be dissociated from the Communist Party in the United States. "The essential fact is the existence of an organization in the United States created by, and completely subservient to, a foreign organization striving to overthrow the existing political and social order in this country. The subversive and pernicious activities of the American Communist Party and the Workers' Party and their subordinate or allied organs in the United States are activities resulting from and flowing out of the program elaborated for them by the Moscow group." With a government committed to such a program the Secretary was unwilling to deal.

Experience seems to indicate that in the long run the course of events and the expediencies of international intercourse will lead to recognition even of a government whose principles are detestable and whose activities are highly objectionable. In the case of Russia the events of 1939 to 1941 would have compelled acknowledgment of the regime in the Kremlin had such action not already been taken. But it would be very hard to show that there was any practical advantage to come from closer association with the Bolshevik regime during the period of Hughes's incumbency at the State Department. And there can be very little doubt that he reflected the majority public opinion of the nation and was free from some of the illusions which the advocates of recognition seem persistently to have cherished.

The position of the Secretary with regard to Russia was

in no way based on hostility to the Russian people. On the contrary, he regarded the situation as one in which "in the absence of a single, recognized Russian government," as he wrote at the time of the Washington Conference, "the protection of legitimate Russian interests must devolve as a moral trusteeship upon the whole" gathering. And, as we have already indicated, in connection with that conference, he exerted some pressure upon the Japanese with regard to the evacuation of Siberia, and was able to get from the Japanese representatives an assurance in this regard. In the same way the State Department hesitated for some time to recognize the governments of the so-called Baltic states which had broken away from Russia in prewar days and had set up independent regimes. Nor did Hughes put any obstacle in the way of the extraordinary program of relief by which the American people came to the aid of the people of Russia in the terrible famine year of 1921.

Hughes and Latin America

The policy of the Secretary with regard to Latin America marks an important stage in the transition from imperialism and offensive measures of control to the policy of the good neighbor, which came to its fruition in the first administration of Franklin D. Roosevelt.

The principles of the Monroe Doctrine, originally intended to prevent European intervention in the affairs of the independent states of the New World, had been twisted in the first sixteen years of the twentieth century into an argument in favor of intervention on the part of the

United States. The argument was not implausible. Some Latin-American states, and particularly the little states in the Caribbean area, by their neglect of their obligations and by the disorder into which they fell, created a situation in which their European creditors might well seek to take some action against them. Was it not right, therefore, in order to forestall such action, for the United States itself to interfere, and set these states in order? Such, at any rate, was the thesis put forward by President Theodore Roosevelt in 1905, and later acted upon by succeeding administrations. Under the Roosevelt corollary, as it was called, American marines landed in Nicaragua in 1912. Strange to say, the Wilson administration, despite its democratic idealism and its anti-imperialistic theory, followed the example set by intervening in the Haitian republic in 1915, and in the Dominican Republic in 1916.

In both of these latter cases there was considerable resistance to the marines, the incidents usual to guerrilla warfare, and a protest from generous-minded Americans. For a time the protest was muffled by the World War, but the criticism became much more vocal in the latter years of Wilson's tenure, and in a mild way, and doubtless without much exact information or reflection on the issue, President Harding made it an issue in the campaign of 1920. The way was prepared, then, for a new policy when Hughes took charge of affairs in March of 1921.

Associated with the Secretary in the first months of office and doubtless exercising an important influence was Sumner Welles. No man was more closely identified with the good-neighbor policy than he. No man had a wider or more sympathetic knowledge of Latin America. Hughes and Welles worked together in forging a new policy, a policy continued after Welles left the department in 1922. In the Dominican Republic, Hughes curbed the Navy dictatorship and suggested the announcement that the United States was ready to turn over the government to the Dominican people as soon as a responsible Dominican Government could be established. Negotiations were long drawn out, but on July 12, 1924, the new regime was actually established, and before autumn was far advanced, the last of the American marines were withdrawn.

This procedure was repeated with regard to Nicaragua. There the case seemed strong for withdrawal since there had been little disorder for many years. The Secretary told the Nicaraguans in November 1923 that after the elections of the next year and the inauguration of the new President the Marine guard at Managua would be brought home. The promise was kept and shortly after the end of Hughes's term the marines were withdrawn. In the case of Haiti, the third Caribbean republic under occupation, a study of the facts convinced Hughes that evacuation would be premature, but the years of his incumbency represent a distinct reaction from the policies that had preceded.

If one looks at the matter more broadly, however, one sees that Hughes's Latin-American attitude stands somewhat between the interventionism of the Taft and Wilson administrations and the treaty pledges against all intervention whatsoever which were to be characteristic of the Franklin Roosevelt administration. Today the United

States stands committed by the protocols of Montevideo and Buenos Aires not to interfere in the domestic affairs of the states of the New World. Hughes never went so far as to advocate such a pledge. He was never ready to agree to a course of action which so severely limited the action of the American Government in the protection of the interests of its citizens. That reluctance was related to his view of the Monroe Doctrine.

The Monroe Doctrine had been the subject of much discussion in connection with the League Covenant. Hughes at the time of the treaty fight had suggested a reservation with regard to it which would have left the solution of New World problems to New World states. He had insisted then, as he was to insist later, upon the fact that the doctrine was a unilateral policy of the United States which it could not submit to international control. "The government of the United States," he wrote in August of 1923, "reserves to itself its definition, interpretation, and application." Having said this, however, Hughes proceeded to dissociate the doctrine from the interventionist policies of preceding administrations. "I utterly disclaim, as unwarranted," he declared in the speech from which we have quoted, "the observations which occasionally have been made implying a claim on our part to superintend the affairs of our sister republics, to assert an overlordship, to consider the spread of our authority beyond our own domain as the aim of our policy and to make our power the test of right in this hemisphere. I oppose all such misconceived and unsound assertions or intimations. They do not express our national purpose; they belie our sincere friendship; they are false to the fundamental principles of our institutions and of our foreign policy which has sought to reflect, with rare exceptions, the ideals of liberty; they menace us by stimulating a distrust which has no real foundation. They find no sanction whatever in the Monroe Doctrine."

This ringing declaration, however, was followed by a careful statement which deprived it of its full force. In the region of the Panama Canal, Hughes went on, the United States had special interests. Its approaches must be protected. Hence in the Caribbean the American Government had to act with all this in view. "The Monroe Doctrine as a particular declaration in no way exhausts American right or policy; the United States has rights and obligations which that Doctrine does not define. And in the unsettled condition of certain countries in the region of the Caribbean it has been necessary to assert these rights and obligations as well as the limited principles of the Monroe Doctrine." Hughes went on to justify what had been done in the Dominican Republic and in Haiti.

In the speech of August 23, the emphasis was on the strategic considerations which might justify action on the part of the United States. But the Secretary was also concerned with the protection of economic interests. He had, as we have seen, been deeply stirred by what he regarded as the laxity of the Wilson administration in dealing with Mexico. His views did not change with his entry into office. He was never completely ready to waive the right of intervention, and he was to demonstrate this somewhat later in his career when he attended the Havana Conference in 1928.

Despite the steps taken by Hughes to allay Latin-American distrust, that distrust continued. At the Fourth Pan-American Conference at Santiago in 1923, Henry Fletcher, the American representative, had many reasons to observe this, and it can hardly be said that his own attitude did much to diminish resentment. Hughes must bear some responsibility for the appointment of a career diplomat who was not very sensitive to the new developments taking place in the field of American diplomacy. The conference appointed a committee of jurists to consider various proposals for the codification of international law, and from the first it was clear that concealed in this innocent-looking proposal was a project to limit the action of the United States.

The years of the Coolidge administration did little to ease matters. We had scarcely withdrawn from Nicaragua before revolution broke out there, and the marines went in again. Secretary Kellogg, in his first years of office, managed to pick a rather serious quarrel with Mexico. Though President Coolidge dealt with this latter situation by the dispatch of Dwight Morrow (a step, it should be said in fairness, suggested by Kellogg himself), irritation with the United States was at white heat when the Havana Conference convened in 1928. Recognizing the gravity of the situation, Hughes was urged to accept the post of chief representative of the United States and, as usual, he accepted the call to public service. No other person could have matched him in prestige.

The great battle at Havana came over the report of the Commission of Jurists. A proposal was put forward in the form of a declaration that "no state may intervene in the internal affairs of another." It was recommended that this proposal be put in the form of a treaty. It was a clear challenge to the United States.

The first discussions on this proposal took part in committee. No fewer than thirteen states rallied to the support of the jurists' declaration. But Hughes fought tenaciously against it, and he was able, as he thought, to secure a postponement of the issue.

But matters turned out a little differently. In the closing session of the conference, Señor Guerrero of El Salvador again raised the critical question. He had not intended to offer a motion for debate, but the chairman misunderstood his observations and requested that he put his views in the form of a motion. As a consequence, what was thought to be no more than a formal closing session became the scene of one of the most exciting debates that had, up to that time, ever taken place in an international body. Delegate after delegate rose to condemn the position of the United States with regard to intervention. The hall rocked with applause. It seemed as if the American Government had been placed in a position from which it would be difficult to extricate itself.

After a long period of discussion, Hughes rose to reply.

His speech was, in the judgment of those present, one of the greatest of his career. He spoke with inward turmoil but with outward self-command. "We do not wish the territory of any American republic," he declared. "We do not wish to govern any American republic. We do not wish to intervene in the affairs of any American republic. We simply wish peace and order and stability and recognition of honest rights properly acquired so that this hemisphere may not only be the hemisphere of peace but the hemisphere of international justice." But "what are we to do," he went on, "when government breaks down and American citizens are in danger of their lives? Are we to stand by and see them butchered in the jungle because a government in circumstances which it cannot control and for which it may not be responsible can no longer afford reasonable protection? . . . It is a principle of international law that in such a case a government is fully justified in taking action — I would call it interposition of a temporary character — for the purpose of protecting the lives and property of its nationals. . . . Of course the United States cannot forego its right to protect its citizens. . . . I cannot sacrifice the rights of my country, but I will join with you in declaring the law. I will try to help you in coming to a just conclusion as to the law; but it must be the law of justice infused with the spirit which has given us from the days of Grotius this wonderful development of the law of nations by which we find ourselves bound."

Once again the galleries responded with applause. And a moment later Guerrero rose and, in a voice that could hardly be heard, withdrew his proposal on the principle that only a unanimous voice could give validity to any resolution of the conference. There seems little doubt that Hughes had won a great forensic victory and won it by the force of his personality and the eloquence of his appeal.

And yet, when the scene at Havana is divested of its drama and when we put away the national feeling to which it so effectively appealed, the "victory" that Hughes won was illusory and his discourse something less than a final statement of an important question. In some respects the speech was rather a lawyer's special plea than an expression of some great and abiding principle. After all, the protection of one's citizens is one thing and the subversion of a native government and the maintenance of external rule for a period of years is something else. And there was an element of semantics in the plea that this was "interposition," not intervention. Furthermore, the general thesis on which Hughes stood at the conference, and which he so ardently and successfully defended, was within a short period of years to be abandoned by the United States.

The truth of the matter is that Hughes was by no means disposed to keep "hands off" in the fullest sense of the word in dealing with Latin America. And, considering his intense criticism of the Wilson administration with regard to Mexico, it is interesting to observe that he himself favored the use of recognition as a moral weapon in dealing with the problems of Central America. The little countries of this area had not been conspicuous for tranquillity at any time, and there was a near flare-up in 1922. Hughes induced the President to call a Central American conference, which met at Washington in December of that same year. The most important achievement of this conference was a treaty by which the five republics concerned pledged themselves "not to aid or recognize any government coming into power in any of the other states by a coup d'état and not to intervene in each other's affairs." The United States was not a signatory to this treaty, but it was taken for granted that it would be bound by its terms. The precedent of 1914, set by Woodrow Wilson with regard to Huerta, was to be followed in Central America. These engagements broke down in 1931 when a revolutionary government came into power in El Salvador, and they were a little later abandoned by the Central American countries themselves. There were other ways in which the policy of moral pressure was used in dealing with the Latin-American states. In Cuba, for instance, scandalous corruption of the Zayas regime had resulted in financial disorganization. Hughes sent to Havana as special ambassador Enoch Crowder, the director of the draft in the First World War. Using to the full the leverage supplied by the Cuban Government's financial embarrassment and its need of a loan to be floated in the United States, Crowder virtually dictated to the lax and corrupt President a program of reform. For a time he had his way, but, the loan once secured, the Cuban Government relapsed into its old bad ways and defied chastisement.

Hughes was more successful in using the power of recognition as a weapon to advance American interests in the case of Mexico. That country, after a turbulent decade, was emerging into relative tranquillity in the twenties. The authority of President Obregon was uncontested. But in a public announcement made on June 7, 1921, Hughes declared that the fundamental question involving American relations with Mexico was "the safeguarding of property rights against confiscation," and went on to imply that the way to recognition was through the negotiation of a satisfactory treaty dealing with the large American oil and agrarian interests in Mexico and with the satisfaction of American claims. He was successful in maintaining this point of view, and in the course of diplomatic conversations an understanding was reached on the questions in dispute and claims conventions negotiated. The Secretary's attitude on this question bears some relationship, as will be perceived, to his attitude towards the Bolshevik regime. It stemmed from his genuine and understandable concern for property rights, but from the Latin-American point of view signing of a treaty of commerce "as an inevitable condition precedent to the extension of recognition to the present government of Mexico" was "prejudicial to the national sovereignty and dignity."

In all the three cases we have mentioned there was much to be said for the point of view which the Secretary assumed. The policy of the good neighbor has not demanded, and should not demand, the abdication of American rights and interests. But it seems fair to say that in the degree to which American influence was exerted, in the emphasis placed on order and on respect for private property, there is a difference between the views of Hughes and the position assumed by later administrations. Perhaps there has been undue tenderness in the treatment of later issues; the decision of this question may be left to the judgment of the reader.

Summary

How shall we sum up Hughes's role in foreign affairs? The writer, before answering the question himself, wishes to refer to a judgment at once more generalized and more specialized. Some years ago he sent to a group of distinguished students of American diplomatic history a list of the Secretaries of State of the United States with the request that these be arranged in order of eminence. There was general agreement that John Quincy Adams should head the list. There was a wide consensus that William H. Seward should come second. But the third man on the list was Charles E. Hughes. Thus, by the judgment of those best qualified to know the facts and most likely to render an objective opinion, Hughes is clearly one of the very most eminent Secretaries.

We may go further and say this. There have been few public officers who so thoroughly dominated their departments and who won a wider measure of admiration from their subordinates. There have been few who were intellectually his equal. There have been few who possessed more technical skill, united with wide imagination, executive force, and genuine idealism. There have been few whose record of accomplishment is more to be admired in relation to the objectives which he set for himself. Almost everything that Hughes tried to do he did, and did well.

Yet we must not fall into indiscriminate eulogy. It was not Hughes's fortune (and the matter is one of the relation of the man to the time) to build long-time policies destined to stand for an age. The great achievement of the Washington treaties collapsed. The reparations settlement of 1924 was revised in 1929. The Latin-American policy he initiated was indeed expanded, but Hughes's defense of American interposition at Havana was outdated by the change in American attitude which came with the non-intervention pledges of 1933 and 1936. There is less left today of his work than of some Secretaries less worthy than he. John Hay, for example, and James G. Blaine have probably left a more enduring mark on American foreign policy.

Nonetheless, no one can review these years without knowing that he has been in touch with a powerful personality, with a public servant of high stature, with a constructive and forward-looking intelligence. And perhaps most important of all is the relationship of Hughes to public opinion. The educational function of a Secretary of State is not the least of his duties. Hughes left office in 1925 having given the American people in many ways a clearer insight of their problems and of the difficulties of solving them in the days ahead.

V I

Hughes as Chief Justice

WHEN HUGHES LAID DOWN HIS CHARGE as Secretary of State in 1925, he naturally stepped into a large law practice and accumulated a substantial fortune. His reputation and capacity were generally recognized. Many wealthy corporations sought him as counsel. In his best year at the bar his income ran as high as $400,000 a year.

But his pecuniary success did not prevent him from rendering public service of many kinds. Of these perhaps the most important was his chairmanship of a Commission for the Reorganization of the Government of the State of New York, a kind of precursor of the Hoover commissions on the national scale. The recommendations made by this commission were, in many instances, carried into effect by Governor Alfred E. Smith and the Republican legislature through nonpartisan effort.

In 1928, Hughes was elected a judge of the Court of International Justice, whose interests he had done so much to promote. His service on this court was to last less than a year and a half, for in 1930 fate intervened. Chief Justice Taft was rapidly declining in health and vigor, and President Hoover was much concerned with the choice of a successor. He turned at once to Hughes, and after ascertaining that the New York lawyer would accept, he sent the nomination to the Senate early in February, 1930. In the perspective of history it is difficult to imagine a better nomination, and such liberal judges as Brandeis of the Supreme Court and Cardozo, then of the New York Court of Appeals, were of this opinion at the time.

Despite this fact, the nomination led to a historic debate which lasted for a week and a half and which finally resulted in the confirmation of the new Chief Justice by a vote of 52 to 26, with more dissenting votes than had been cast in many years on a judicial appointment.

What was behind this extraordinary exhibition? The heart of the matter appears to lie in the fact that the Senators were emphasizing, as it had never been emphasized before, the fact that the Supreme Court is a great political as well as a great judicial agency, and that, as we have seen in an earlier chapter, the social and economic predilections of the judges have something to do with the opinions that they hand down. This was an important public service. In the judgment of the writer, there is no impropriety whatsoever in scrutinizing the previous record of a candidate for the highest judicial office in the land.

It is a wholly different question whether or not anything in Hughes's past justified a negative vote on the issue of confirmation. The criticisms leveled against him were of two sorts. One had to do with his partisan activity. Senator Norris was disturbed not so much at the idea of Hughes's leaving the bench in 1916, as at his being about to return to it after considerable participation in Republican politics. Hughes had spoken — and spoken frequently — in defense of the Harding and Coolidge administrations, and he had warmly espoused the candidacy of President Hoover in 1928. In some of these speeches, as is to be expected of virtually any partisan speech, there was special pleading. But other judges of the Supreme Court, including the great John Marshall himself, or his successor, Roger Taney, were not detached from party affairs, and both of them amply vindicated themselves upon the bench. More important, perhaps, the opponents of the Hughes nomination laid considerable stress upon the character of his clients in the years when he was most active at the bar. Many of these, as has already been said, had been corporations of great size. Criticism turned particularly on two of these, the Oil Institute of America and the General Electric Company. In the first case, attention was called to the fact that such unsavory characters as Sinclair and Doheny, who had figured prominently in the oil scandals of the Harding administration, were members of the governing board. In the second, Hughes had argued that the General Electric Company, operating radio station WGY, had acquired a vested interest in the transmission channel it was using. Was it certain, it was asked, that the judge on the bench could divorce himself from sympathy with vested interests after defending them as an attorney?

The answer to this question, as attested by the Chief Justice's later career and by his salient traits of character, is certainly in the affirmative. The Hughes of the period 1930–1944 may have been more conservative than the Hughes of the period 1910–1916, but no fair-minded person can possibly view him on the bench as the blind advocate of corporate interests. Hughes was extremely austere in reconciling his public with his private role. He came near to snubbing Chief Justice Taft when Taft greeted him cordially on his first appearance as an attorney before the Court. When Charles E. Hughes, Jr., was named Solicitor General in 1927, his father refused to appear on the other side in cases where young Charles represented the government. He would have nothing to do with arguing for a proposition which he had already decided against on the bench. In general he would not put his name on a brief for which he did not assume full responsibility. He would not represent foreign interests with claims against the United States, since his special knowledge of our foreign relations might inadvertently advantage such clients. And while his practice was largely corporate, in at least one highly important case, the case of the coal miners, he championed the cause of labor.

But there was a larger question involved than the question of Hughes's personal principles. It is by no means necessarily true that a great lawyer loses the capacity for objective thinking in successful practice. Some of them may, but others may not. Many matters of law are delicately poised. Each point of view deserves to be stated as effectively as possible. Because a man argues well for a private client, it is not at all to be taken for granted that he will not protect the public interest when placed upon the bench, or will be unduly influenced by his previous associations. The argument that no highly successful advocate ought ever to be placed upon the Supreme Court was certainly not justified in the case of Charles Evans Hughes. Had it been so, such men as Brandeis and Cardozo would not have applauded the nomination.

Hughes was painfully affected by the debate on his confirmation. He had wished to avoid a political wrangle, and was unhappy that such a wrangle occurred. But he held his peace, and on February 24 he took the oath as Chief Justice of the United States. He was to serve in that capacity for more than ten years.

Both the bench and the social circumstances of 1930 were far different from those of 1910. In 1910 the judges, as we have seen, had been, on the whole, remarkably united in their judgment on the most fundamental questions that came before them. The atmosphere of the Court was relatively tranquil. Though there were stirrings of social change, as illustrated by the Progressive movement, there was no acute economic situation to sharpen political antagonisms.

In 1930 the situation was otherwise. At the outset of Hughes's term, the nation had already entered the period of the Great Depression. Mounting unemployment, agrarian unrest, tension among the workers, all produced a social situation that was grave in the extreme. The remedies proposed by the Roosevelt administration were bound to divide opinion and to exacerbate political and social cleavages. At such a time it is not strange that the differences in outlook felt in the nation as a whole should appear in the Court, as they had in the days of the slavery controversy. Hughes had to grapple, as time went on, with a kind of unyielding conservatism on the part of four of his colleagues, Butler, McReynolds, Van Devanter, and Sutherland. He faced a problem in judicial statesmanship that was almost overwhelming.

Hughes knew that a divided Court is a Court which loses public confidence. But he had a deep respect for his colleagues, and he did not like to think in terms of judicial blocs. The four conservatives became in this period closely united, often coming to the Court together and concerting their views before the judicial conference. It would have been alien to the nature of the Chief Justice to try to form a similar group in opposition to them. His conception of the office and his notions of judicial propriety forbade it.

If Hughes could not unify the Court, he could and did immensely increase its efficiency. His powerful administrative instincts found expression in important reforms. It was at his urging that the Court adopted in 1938 new rules of civil procedure which immensely simplified the administration of justice. He made effective efforts to expedite the work of the lower courts. He had a significant part in the framing of the important statute of 1939 which created the Administrative Office of the United States Courts, which operates under the Conference of Senior

Circuit Judges. This agency has done important work in supervising the lower courts and speeding up the course of justice. No Chief Justice showed more executive talent than Hughes; none realized more acutely that the delay of justice is often its denial.

In turning to the analysis of Hughes's judicial service in detail, we may well begin by considering his attitude towards the growth of federal power. In general he was to look favorably upon such growth, as he had in his previous term on the bench. At the very beginning of his service, for example, he spoke for the Court in deciding that an act designed to protect the rights of interstate railway employees to organize was constitutional. He held that this right extended even to railway clerks who were not directly engaged in interstate commerce. In a second railroad case, involving the constitutionality of a federal statute establishing a compulsory retirement and pension system for carriers, he dissented vigorously from the decision of the majority judges which struck down the law. In still a third case, and one of great significance, he upheld the power of Congress to reassign radio frequencies.

He took a similarly broad view in the case of *Ashwander v. Tennessee Valley Authority*. This case, touching the constitutionality of the Tennessee Valley Authority and its right to dispose of the electrical energy generated at the dams, involved much more than the commerce power. But the construction of the dams, the Chief Justice held, was legitimately based in part upon that power.

But, in common with all his colleagues, he reacted

against the sweeping extension of the commerce clause that seemed to him at issue in the Schechter case arising under the National Industrial Recovery Act. This famous statute authorized the setting up of codes in the various fields of industry. These codes regulated prices, conditions of employment, and commercial practices in a vast variety of businesses, one of which was live poultry. The Schechter firm was so engaged, but almost exclusively in buying and selling poultry in the City of New York. When charged with violation of the codes, it had recourse to the courts, and the case came before Hughes and his colleagues in 1935. By a unanimous vote the Court set aside the law, and it was Hughes who rendered judgment.

In so doing, he entered into detailed discussion of the commerce clause. "The power of Congress," he wrote, with an eye to his own past decisions, "extends not only to the regulation of transactions which are a part of interstate commerce, but to the protection of that commerce from injury. It matters not that the injury may be due to the conduct of those engaged in intra-state operations. But," he went on, "there is a necessary and well-established distinction between direct and indirect effects. If the commerce clause were construed to reach all enterprises and transactions which could be said to have an indirect effect upon interstate commerce, the federal authority would embrace practically all the activities of the people and the authority of the State over its domestic concerns would exist only by sufferance of the federal government." The Chief Justice's point of view was supported by Mr. Justice

Cardozo in a concurring opinion. Essentially what was argued was that the code system, in its manifestation, so far obliterated the distinction between federal and state control as to fall under the ban of the Constitution.

The reasoning of the Chief Justice in the Schechter case has been subjected to substantial criticism by distinguished students of constitutional law and is not beyond cavil. In specific terms, however, there seems to this author much to be said for it, since the Recovery Act explicitly dealt with violations of the codes "in any transaction in or affecting interstate commerce," and since the sale of live poultry in the City of New York might reasonably be held to involve no such transaction. But the more generalized language of the decision, with its attempt to distinguish between the direct and indirect effects on commerce of federal legislation, raises some very difficult questions, and opens the door to distinctions which, as Justice Stone put it, are "too mechanical, too uncertain in application, and too remote from actualities, to be of value."

Hughes took a somewhat different ground in dealing with the Bituminous Coal Conservation Act of 1935. This act levied a tax on bituminous coal with a drawback of 90 per cent to those producers who conformed to certain standards with regard to hours of labor and to wages. At the same time it fixed minimum and maximum prices. The Chief Justice was one of four dissenting justices who thought that the price-fixing provisions should be sustained. In an individual opinion, somewhat paralleling the dissent of Justices Cardozo, Brandeis, and Stone, he pointed out that the language of the statute specifically stipulated that the provisions dealing with prices should be considered as separable from the rest of the act and that on this basis they might be sustained as relating to "marketing in interstate commerce." But he acquiesced in Justice Sutherland's opinion which found that the wage and hour prescriptions of the act were unconstitutional. Though the record was, in the words of a distinguished student of constitutional law, "replete with evidences of the effects of this part of the statute on interstate commerce," he raised no objection to the prescriptions' being set aside.

Within less than a year, however, he took advanced ground on another statute of far-reaching consequence involving the interests of the worker. In the interval President Roosevelt had been re-elected overwhelmingly and had brought forward his famous proposal for the reconstruction of the Court. Whether this had or had not anything to do with the shift in Hughes's attitude is, in the case of a man so discreet as Hughes, a matter on which it is distinctly unwise to be dogmatic. The case in question involved the constitutionality of the Wagner Labor Relations Act, which brought collective bargaining under federal regulation and control on an unprecedented scale. In a five-to-four decision the Chief Justice sustained the legislation. He was not deterred from doing so by the claim that the statute's effect on interstate commerce was indirect. On the contrary, he took the position that there could be no logical ground for setting aside the law on the basis of its purely local influence. "It is idle," he wrote, "to say that the effect would be indirect or remote. It is obvious that it would be immediate and catastrophic. We are asked to shut our eyes to the plainest facts of our national life and to deal with the question of direct and indirect effects in an intellectual vacuum. . . . When industries organize themselves on a national scale, making their relation to interstate commerce the dominant factor in their activities, how can it be maintained that their industrial relations constitute a forbidden field into which Congress may not enter when it is necessary to protect interstate commerce from the paralyzing consequences of industrial war?" Such language, however motivated, brings us back to the Hughes who wrote the Shreveport decision twenty-six years before.

The decision in the Wagner Act opened the way to many others of tremendous importance. As Professor Hendel justly says, "They [these further cases] placed the regulation of the relationships between capital and labor clearly within the province of governmental power, national and state, and thereby struck another blow at the laissez-faire conception of liberty under due process which had so long held dominance in the Court." They paved the way for the approval of further regulatory legislation in the field of wages and hours. The act of 1938, prescribing minimum wages and maximum hours, was declared constitutional in 1941 by a court no longer divided on the issue.

The commerce clause figured also in two other important decisions affecting the legislation of the Roosevelt era. It was used in 1939 to sustain the Holding Companies Act in a decision rendered by the Chief Justice himself, and approved by all but one of his colleagues. And it played an important part in the validation of the Agricultural Adjustment Act in 1937. In this latter case, it permitted the imposition by the federal government of quotas for the marketing of certain designated crops, and the imposition of a fine on the warehouseman who accepted tobacco beyond the prescribed quotas. Wonderful indeed is what can be done where the will exists in enlarging the powers of the federal government through those innocent little words, "to regulate commerce." In all these cases, whether he handed down the decision or not, Hughes took the broad and not the narrow view. His vote was cast on the side of wide, not narrow, national authority.

It was not only the construction of the commerce clause that raised, in the Hughes Court, important questions of national power. In an entirely different category, for example, were the cases involving the devaluation of the dollar. In the distressful conditions of 1933, Congress authorized the President to decrease the gold value of our standard unit of currency by 49.94 per cent. The President did so, and his action gave rise to a series of lawsuits involving both private and public contracts in which payment of debts was stipulated in fixed terms of the currency in relation to gold. In a very close decision, by a vote of five to four, the Court sustained the government's action unequivocally with regard to private contracts, on the ground that the Constitution had given to Congress "broad and comprehensive national authority" over the subjects of revenue, finance, and currency. "Parties," wrote the Chief Justice, "cannot remove their transactions from the reach of dominant constitutional power by making contracts about them." The Court might, of course, in any given case, decide to examine the question whether there was a deprivation of property without due process of law, or whether the action taken bore a reasonable relation to a legitimate end. But, "if it is an appropriate means to such an end, the decision of Congress as to the final degree of the necessity for the adoption of that means is final."

The Chief Justice had more difficulty, however, in deciding whether the gold clause in *public* contracts, that is, in government bonds, was equally subordinate to the action of the legislature. Here, the conservative justices maintained, was a clear violation of a contract, and thus a deprivation of property without due process of law. In dealing with this question, Hughes performed what can only be regarded as a remarkable feat of judicial legerdemain. The gold clause on government bonds was, he declared, "binding upon the conscience of the sovereign," and the congressional legislation with regard to the devaluation of the dollar was, to that degree, "beyond Congressional power." So far, so good. But, the Chief Justice went on, the question of damage was "a distinct question." Considering the practical situation, to repay the face value of the bond in terms of gold "would appear to constitute not a recoupment of loss in any proper sense, but an unjustified enrichment." This ingenious formula did not satisfy Mr. Justice Stone, who went the limit in asserting the supremacy of governmental power over the contractual obligation written into the bond, but three of the Justice's colleagues, Cardozo, Brandeis, and Roberts, went along with this rather sophistical reasoning, and the Roosevelt administration was thus narrowly preserved from serious embarrassment.

It was not thus in the very extraordinary case involving the Agricultural Adjustment Act of 1935. At issue was the validity of a processing tax laid on certain agricultural commodities, the proceeds thereof to be paid to farmers who reduced their acreage in accordance with a preconceived plan. On this occasion, the Chief Justice associated himself with five other justices, Sutherland, Van Devanter, Butler, McReynolds, and Roberts, in asserting the invalidity of such legislation.

In some respects it is difficult to reconcile Hughes's participation in this decision with his general judicial philosophy. Justice Roberts, who delivered the opinion, went at times pretty far in asserting doctrines that were in the way of abandonment. He trotted out the hoary generalization that the Court had no real power of choice, but merely laid the statute alongside the Constitution and came to an inevitable result — not so inevitable, however, that three justices did not dissent. In flat disregard of Hughes's general predilections, he invoked the old doctrine that the Tenth Amendment, in reserving the rights of the states, somehow excluded the federal government from some fields altogether. And categorically he stated, "Congress has no power to enforce its commands on the farmer to the ends sought by the Agricultural Adjustment Act," a statement which went far beyond the bounds of judicial necessity. This, too, was hardly in the Hughes spirit.

But there was a saving paragraph in the Roberts opinion to which Hughes attributed great importance, and which influenced him in aligning himself with the majority. This was the assertion that the taxing power could be exercised under the "general welfare" clause of the Constitution, and "that the power of Congress to authorize expenditure of public moneys for public purposes is not limited by the direct grants of legislative power found in the Constitution." This paragraph was extremely useful at a later date when the Court acted on the social-security legislation and declared such legislation valid by a close vote.

Nonetheless, in no decision of the Court did Hughes so clearly associate himself with the conservative members as against the apostles of a broad construction of our fundamental law. It may well be that he was influenced by a desire to avoid a five-to-four decision at a time when the Court was under criticism.

Much more easily explained is his attitude towards features of the National Industrial Recovery Act not subsumed under the commerce clause. The Chief Justice reacted strongly against the possible abuse of administrative power. He had been a partisan of such power within defined limits; he now feared, very definitely, that that power might be abused. Early in his career Hughes had understood the danger that the courts might hamstring the administrative process; now he perceived also the danger that administrative process might become arbitrary and capricious, denying the citizen his fundamental rights. He therefore found the code-fixing authority of the National Industrial Recovery Act a dangerous delegation of power to the executive and to the members of an industry to make rules for all their members under executive authority. In basing his decision in the famous Schechter case on these grounds, he was, after all, expressing not only his own point of view, but the point of view of all the members of the Court. There were limits to the degree to which Congress could hand over its lawmaking functions to others. All nine of the judges believed these limits had been exceeded in the N.R.A.

More questionable — certainly more critically viewed by distinguished students of the problem — was the attitude of the Chief Justice in other questions involving the rights and duties of administrative tribunals. Early in his term he carried the Court with him in a case, decided six to three, in which the principle that questions of fact might be finally considered by an administrative tribunal was, to use Professor Hendel's language, "seriously disturbed." In another case he went with the majority in a singularly emotional decision in which the Court declared that the Securities Exchange Commission could not proceed to ascertain the facts in a registration statement after that statement had been discovered to be fraudulent and had been withdrawn. In still another instance Hughes stated the doctrine of judicial review with regard to the fixing of rates for certain services regulated under the Packers and Stockyards Act in such terms as to provoke dissent from Stone, Brandeis, and Cardozo. And in a fourth matter he declared invalid a hearing under this act because it did not accord with his conceptions of reasonable investigation and was not rendered "in accordance with the cherished judicial tradition embodying the basic concepts of fair play."

It is possible to understand and to sympathize with Hughes's desire to "judicialize" administrative power. He stated his ideal in one of the cases cited above. "The multiplication of administrative agencies is the outstanding characteristic of our time. The controversies within the range of administrative action may be different and extremely important, and they may call for a particular type of experience and special methods of inquiry, but the spirit which should animate that action, if the authority is to be properly exercised, must be the spirit of the just judge." Nonetheless, in some instances at least, Hughes seems to have adopted a point of view which would substantially interfere with the efficiency of the administrative or regulatory process.

Let us turn from our examination of the attitude of the Chief Justice towards federal power and examine his attitude towards the exercise of legislative power by the states. We have already seen how the due-process clause and, in a less degree, the "equal protection of the laws" clause of the Fourteenth Amendment had long been used to curtail the action of state legislatures in dealing with economic and social problems. We have seen, too, how as early as the period of Hughes's first term on the Court, and to no small degree under the influence of Justice Holmes, the judicial doctrine was undergoing modification. We have seen that Hughes himself took a liberal, rather than a restricted, view of state power. He continued to do so, in the main, in the period of his Chief Justiceship.

If we turn to the examination of the most important specific cases, the record stands somewhat as follows. Hughes joined five other judges in 1932 in declaring unconstitutional an Oklahoma statute which required a license for the manufacturing and selling of ice. But in 1934, in a five to four decision, he stood with the majority of the Court in upholding the validity of a New York statute fixing maximum and minimum prices for the sale of milk. He was one of four dissenting judges in the case of *Morehead v. Tipaldo,* in which the Court held unconstitutional a minimum wage law for women enacted by the state of New York. In 1937 he spoke for a majority of the Court in a case involving a Washington statute in which a minimum-wage law was upheld. In this case, indeed, he not only overcame a characteristic reluctance directly to overrule a previous decision, but, what was perhaps more important, he indicated in the course of his opinion that "economic circumstances had supervened" which made this reversal desirable. This mode of argument caused much anguish to four of his colleagues, Butler, Mc-

Reynolds, Van Devanter, and Sutherland. "The meaning of the Constitution," wrote the last-named, "does not change with the ebb and flow of economic events." In the difference between the Chief Justice and his four conservative associates was sharply etched one of the great issues which divides the judges known as liberal from those known as conservative. Even though one admits that the language of the Constitution with regard to due process must be interpreted by some standard of "reasonableness," does not — should not — this standard change from age to age? Hughes answered this question in the affirmative.

More epoch-making than any of these decision in its broad implications is the decision of the divided Court, the four conservatives again dissenting, in the Minnesota moratorium cases. The Minnesota statute challenged in these cases provided that during a declared emergency lasting for a period of two years foreclosures might be postponed and periods of redemption of mortgages extended. This could only be done, however, after application to the courts, and only on condition that the debtor pay a determined part of the reasonable value of the rental of the property, or a reasonable part of the income derived from such property. In other words, the enactment, while recognizing the hardship of the debtor, attempted at the same time to take account of the interest of the creditor, and provided for judicial reconciliation of these conflicting interests at a time of general distress.

Now, the "impairment of contracts" clause had usually been rigorously interpreted by the Court insofar as private contracts were concerned, except in regard to leases following the First World War, when a housing shortage led to both state and federal legislation depriving the lessor of some of his ordinary rights. It was not strange, therefore, that the conservative members of the Court were not favorable to the Minnesota statute. But Hughes, with the support of four other judges, not only found the law constitutional but also, citing the precedents of the housing cases, went on to provide a broader basis for the validity of the act.

In language that has met with some criticism he attempted to generalize in a way which provoked Mr. Justice Sutherland to animated protest. Hughes declared that while "emergency does not create power, emergency may furnish the occasion for the exercise of power," a cryptic phrase which the dissenting judge considered mere semantics. Hughes went on to deny that "what the Constitution meant to the vision of that day it must mean to the vision of our time. If by the statement that what the Constitution meant at the time of its adoption it means today, it is intended to say that the great clauses of the Constitution must be confined to the interpretation which the framers, with the conditions and outlook of their time, would have placed upon them, the statement carries its own refutation." And he proceeded to read the impairment of contracts clause, the qualification of a latent police power. "The reservation of essential aspects of sovereign power is read into contracts as a postulate of the legal order. The policy of protecting contracts against impairment presupposes the maintenance of a government by virtue of which contractual relations are worth while — a government which retains adequate authority to secure the peace and good order of society." He declared also that "when the fundamental interests of the state are affected, the question is no longer merely that of one party to a contract as against another but of the use of reasonable means to safeguard the economic structure upon which the good of all depends." It is hardly necessary to emphasize the sweeping character of this language or to point out what wide latitude it might give for emergency legislation. In some ways it hardly seems characteristic of the Chief Justice. And whatever else may or may not be said of it, it certainly demonstrated that Hughes in 1934 was very far from that encrusted conservatism which distinguished some members of the Court.

On one matter involving due process Hughes stood with all his brethren in interpreting restrictively the due-process clause. There came before the Court in 1933 a case involving the rights of a state governor under martial law. The governor of Texas, having declared martial law, had proceeded by virtue of this declaration to fix maximum limits of oil production within the state, and to enforce these limits by military authority. His action was declared unconstitutional in the case of *Sterling v. Constantin.* "Where there is a substantial showing that the exertion of state power has overridden private rights secured by the Constitution," wrote the Chief Justice, "the subject is necessarily one for judicial inquiry in an appropriate proceeding directed against the individuals charged with the transgression." While this case was criticized at the time, it is certainly most debatable whether the exercise of the power to declare martial law, and to act under it, ought not to be restricted by the courts. The Hughes decision did not involve a point of view at all reactionary.

We must next examine the attitude of the Chief Justice towards a long-standing doctrine of the Court which exempted from state taxation the instrumentalities of the federal government, and from federal taxation, *per contra,* the instrumentalities of the state. In a period when the fiscal necessities of both state and federal regimes were increasing there was a strong case for a narrow interpretation of this rule. On the other hand, powerful precedents stood in the way. Hughes hesitated to break with the past; yet he saw and understood the character of the problem. In the two most important cases in which he spoke for the Court he took the broad view. And it is also true that during his Chief Justiceship the Court in general liberalized its rules on this matter without at any time provoking the dissent of the Chief Justice. The net result was a substantial limitation of the doctrine of immunity and a wider sphere for state and federal taxation.

We must close our discussion of the philosophy of the Chief Justice with an examination of his position on cases involving racial discrimination and intellectual liberty. We have seen how in his first term of service Hughes reacted to the Alabama statute which seemed to him to smack of peonage. In his tenure as Chief Justice he showed a similar solicitude for the rights of the Negro.

Hughes rendered his greatest service in connection with the Scottsboro cases. A group of Negroes who were charged with rape had been tried under conditions which made conviction certain. In the first trial no real attempt was made to provide them with adequate counsel, and the Court set aside their conviction on this ground. In the second trial, in the case of *Norris v. Alabama,* the Court once again decided that due process had been violated, this time because Negroes were excluded from the jury. Going beyond concrete evidence of exclusion in the specific sense, it examined the general situation prevailing in the county in which the alleged criminals were tried. In still another case involving one of the defendants the Court advanced even further. Setting aside the general rule that it does not re-examine a question of appellate state procedure, it went at length into the circumstances under which the appeal of one of the defendants was denied in the state court and remanded the case to the court below. To put the matter succinctly, Hughes was determined to go beyond the forms and look to the facts in connection with the rights of the humblest citizens.

The problem of segregation in the schools was handled in the same spirit. In 1896 the judicial rule of equal but separate accommodations had been set up by the Court in the case of *Plessy v. Ferguson.* Insofar as education was concerned, the first breach in the rule — later to be discarded altogether — was made by the Hughes Court in the case of *Missouri ex. rel. Gaines v. Canada,* which held that a properly qualified Negro must be admitted to the law school of the University of Missouri, and that it was not a fulfillment of the constitutional guarantee of "equal protection of the laws" if his tuition were paid in a law school in some other state. Hughes was able to carry with him in this decision only four of the justices. But in another case, involving the question of a Negro who had purchased a first-class railway ticket and was compelled to ride in a second-class car, Hughes was able to speak for all his brethren. Not only this but the language of his decision suggests that, while this case was decided under the "equal protection" clause of the Fourteenth Amendment, the Chief Justice was ready to take a similar position with regard to federal legislation under the due-process clause. It should perhaps also be observed that the Court which gave unanimous support to Hughes's position in this case was the Court as reconstituted after the great constitutional battle of 1937.

In suffrage cases the role of the Hughes Court in preventing discrimination against Negroes was less fundamental, yet important. The Southern states had resorted to various forms of chicanery to deprive the Negro of the suffrage guaranteed him by the Fifteenth Amendment. One of these devices was the grandfather clause, which excluded from the suffrage certain classes of voters unless their parents or grandparents had voted prior to the adoption of the amendment. This clause had been held unconstitutional in 1915. A palpable attempt to evade this decision was set aside by the Court in 1941. In another case Justice Cardozo, speaking for the majority of the justices, declared unconstitutional a statute in which Negroes were barred from voting in Democratic primaries in the state of Texas. But when the statute was repealed and the Democratic Party of Texas again excluded Negroes, this time acting as a mere association of individuals without legal status, the Court found it impossible to interfere. While significant steps were taken towards preventing the Negro from being excluded from the polls, the problem was by no means solved. It is again worth noting that such progress as was made was made over the opposition of Justices Butler, McReynolds, Sutherland, and Van Devanter.

In taking the position that he did with regard to the rights of the Negro, Hughes was merely expressing the philosophy that he had already advocated when he was Associate Justice. And the same thing can be said of his attitude towards freedom of speech and association. Hughes believed that tolerance was the hallmark of a democratic society. He had demonstrated the depth and intensity of his conviction in 1920 upon the expulsion of the Socialist members from the New York Assembly; and he did not change his views. As Chief Justice he was almost invariably on the side of freedom. He took a more restrictive view of constitutional guarantees only in the Gobitis case, in which the Court, speaking through Justice Frankfurter, and with only Justice Stone dissenting, held constitutional the expulsion of two children from the public schools for refusal, on religious grounds, to salute the flag. In the main he was the clear-voiced defender of intellectual and religious liberty.

A series of cases involved religious freedom. In one the issue was whether a professor of theology at Yale University, who had applied for naturalization papers, should be denied citizenship because he had, in making his application, indicated that while he was not opposed to all wars, he would not support a war that went against his conscience. The Court, by a five to four vote, decided against the applicant. But the Chief Justice wrote the dissenting opinion, and was supported by three other justices. "The battle for religious liberty has been fought and won," he wrote, in one of his greatest opinions, "with respect to religious beliefs and practices, which are not in conflict with good order, upon the very ground of the supremacy of conscience within its proper field. . . . There is abundant reason for enforcing the requisite authority of law . . . without demanding that either citizens or applicants for citizenship shall assume by oath an obligation to regard allegiance to God as subordinate to allegiance to civil power."

In two cases involving the sect known as Jehovah's Witnesses, Hughes again showed his concern for religious freedom. In one he set aside a statute, violated by members of this sect, which forbade the distribution of literature of any kind within the limits of the city of Griffin without first obtaining the written permission of the city manager. In another he associated himself with a decision by Justice Roberts which invalidated a state law which forbade solicitation for religious or charitable purposes without the approval of a public-welfare official.

Hughes also wrote a weighty decision sustaining the freedom of the press. A Minnesota statute provided for the abatement, as a public nuisance, of a "malicious, scandalous and defamatory newspaper, magazine or other periodical." The statute was claimed to have been violated by a highly sensational newspaper which charged that outrageous conditions existed with regard to bootlegging and racketeering in the city of Minneapolis. Here was involved not the possibility of an action for libel but the suppression, by injunction, of a sheet which flouted the law. "The fact that liberty of the press may be abused by miscreant purveyors of scandal," wrote the Chief Justice, speaking for a divided Court, "does not make any less necessary the immunity of the press from previous restraints in dealing with official misconduct." Such restraints he declared "to be of the essence of censorship." In this decision Hughes perhaps did more to affirm the liberty of the press than any justice in the history of the Court.

In several interesting cases, and consistently with his previously held views as to the place of labor in society, Hughes gave wide scope to the activities of labor unions. He joined, for example, in declaring unconstitutional a law which prohibited peaceful picketing, and in two other cases concurred in opinions which brought the right of such picketing within the scope of liberty protected by the Fourteenth Amendment. When Jersey City enacted an ordinance prohibiting assemblies upon the public streets, highways, or parks without a permit, an ordinance directed against the C.I.O. by that extraordinary figure Mayor Hague, the Chief Justice joined the majority of the Court in setting it aside. There were limits, however, beyond which he would not go. He would not sanction picketing when "enmeshed" with violence, and he refused to accept the majority view that it could not be enjoined when directed against a concern in which there was no labor dispute between employer and employees, and no desire to join a union.

If, in these latter cases, the Chief Justice seems to some minds to have moved towards the right, this impression will most certainly be modified by his decisions in cases involving revolutionary agitation. *Stromberg v. California* arose from a California statute which "forbade the display of a red flag as a sign, symbol, or emblem of opposition to organized government, or as an invitation or stimulus to anarchistic action, or finally as an aid to propaganda that is of a seditious character." A violation of this statute was charged to a young girl, admittedly Communist in sympathy, who was acting as one of the supervisors of a young people's camp in which the children were taught the solidarity of the laboring class and in which the red flag was daily saluted. There was no proof of any direct incitement to violence. Hughes carried with him six of his brethren in declaring the statute unconstitutional on the ground that the first of the three clauses cited, the display of the flag as "a symbol of opposition to organized government," was too vague to be regarded as a legitimate prohibition, and that as it might well have been the basis of the previous conviction of the appellant, the conviction must be reversed.

Another case brought an Oregon statute into question. This statute made it a criminal offense to assist in the conduct of a meeting called by any organization advocating criminal syndicalism or sabotage. One De Jonge, himself a Communist, took part in an orderly meeting of protest directed against illegal raids on workers' halls and the shooting of striking longshoremen and police. He was arrested under the statute and convicted. The Supreme Court set aside his conviction on the ground that the law was a deprivation of liberty since it made merely assisting in the preparation of a legal assemblage, if that assemblage were called by a criminal organization, itself criminal. In other words, Hughes dealt an emphatic blow against the principle of guilt by association, which is one of the favorite weapons of the more infuriated Red-hunters.

In still a third question that came before the Court, decided by a five to four vote, Hughes associated himself with a broad view of civil rights. Herndon, a Negro, and a paid organizer of the Communist Party, had been convicted under a pre-Civil War Georgia statute for attempting to incite insurrection. He had in his possession a booklet which advocated a revolutionary struggle for power "even if the situation does not yet warrant the raising of the question of uprising." Justice Roberts delivered the decision of the Court. Rejecting the view that a dangerous tendency might be made the standard of guilt, he declared that "penalizing even of utterances of a defined character must find its justification in a reasonable apprehension of danger to organized government." The statute, he declared, was "so vague and indefinite" that it afforded no standard by which to judge of the existence of "a clear and present danger of forcible obstruction of a particular state function" and thus violated the guarantee of liberty embodied in the Fourteenth Amendment.

When one surveys as a whole the record of the Chief Justice on these civil liberty cases, one agrees with Professor Hendel, a distinguished student of the matter, that Hughes had a "greater fondness for the Bill of Rights than any other Chief Justice." The decisions in which he participated came at a time when the specter of totalitarianism in Europe loomed larger than ever but before the public mind had become infected with the fear that the institutions of this country were threatened with a terrible danger of internal subversion. He set up a standard in these decisions to which later generations might well repair.

It has been essential to the understanding of our subject to trace the opinions of Hughes on the bench, and these in specific terms. Yet we ought not to allow this necessary preoccupation to bar us from broad generalization with regard to the attitude of the Chief Justice. What is to be said of him from this larger point of view? In general Hughes displayed as Chief Justice a kind of balance characteristic of the best judicial mind. He was keenly aware of the value of precedent, and sometimes he strained logic a bit in avoiding outright reversal of previous cases. But he was far removed from that blind adherence to the past that characterized such a justice as McReynolds and to a lesser degree some of his brethren. Hughes believed in the function of the Court as a balance wheel of the Constitution. But he was by no means one of those who wished to use the judicial veto to arrest the social tendencies of the time and the course of democratic government. In many decisions, of lesser importance than the key ones that we have cited, he often took the conservative side; in major matters he exerted a liberal leadership. It has sometimes been made a matter of reproach to him that he more often assigned to himself the writing of the Court's opinion when it was moving forward than when it was standing still, more often when it was liberal than when it was conservative. But should not this have been the case? Should not the authority of the Chief Justice as spokesman be used to affirm the flexibility of the law, rather than its dependence on precedent? Was not Hughes thus playing the role of a judicial statesman? The answer of this writer would be in the affirmative. But we shall be able to judge more accurately the Chief Justice's judicial statesmanship if we turn to the role he played in the historic controversy over the composition of the Court which broke upon the nation in 1937.

VII
The Court Struggle

By far the most important chapter in Hughes's Chief Justiceship concerns the struggle over the composition of the Court in 1937. This was, of course, not the first sharp conflict between the executive and the judiciary in the history of the United States. Indeed, the Presidents commonly regarded as our greatest, with the exception of Washington, who appointed the whole Court, have all in one way or another had their moments of stress with the judicial power. Jefferson encouraged the use of the machinery of impeachment against a partisan judge and might, had he succeeeded, have extended it to others. Jackson is reported to have said with regard to the decision of the tribunal in an Indian case, "John Marshall has made his decision. Now let him enforce it." Lincoln was sharply critical of the Dred Scott decision affirming the constitutionality of slavery in the territories and even charged that there was a conspiracy between the judges and the executive. Theodore Roosevelt expressed more than once his impatience with judicial logic and, on the state level, proposed the recall of judicial decisions. And Woodrow Wilson faced a bitter political battle in attempting to place on the Court a great liberal lawyer, Louis D. Brandeis, as a kind of antidote to its natural conservatism. The struggle during the term of F. D. Roosevelt was only the latest, and perhaps the most dramatic, in a series of conflicts between the executive and the judiciary that run through the constitutional history of the United States.

All involved the same principle. The Court, as we have seen, is inevitably a political as well as a judicial body. If its decisions run counter to the prevailing opinion of the country, there is bound to be criticism. If these decisions are rendered by a divided tribunal, the criticism is bound to be intensified. The American people, as the struggle of 1937 showed, are in general definitely favorable to the principle of judicial review. But at the same time a considerable part of them become impatient when the Court stands in the way of what they consider to be necessary changes in the political and social order, especially when it is clear, as it is in decisions by a divided court, that the questions involved are susceptible of an interpretation more favorable to social and economic adjustment.

There are a number of judicial decisions that play a crucial part in the events of 1937. First we may mention again the gold-clause cases. Here the judgment was favorable to the administration, but only by a five to four vote; and the consequences of a contrary decision, it is not too much to say, would have plunged the country into confusion, since the statute involved had been in force for more than two years. Furthermore, the tone of that part of the decision which referred to public contracts and implied a breach of faith was warmly resented by the administration. Next came the Railroad Retirement Act case. Here again was a five to four decision, this time against the government; and here again the language of the majority judges was irritating since it suggested a further curtailment of federal power. Only three weeks later came three more decisions highly distasteful to the administration. The first declared invalid the Frazier-Lemke Act to relieve agricultural debtors. The second restricted the power of the President to remove the members of regulatory commissions when he was out of sympathy with their point of view. The third laid low the National Industrial Recovery Act.

Each of these three decisions, it should be noted, was unanimous. The fact should make us pause in condemning them. In each case there was an excellent judicial argument for the point of view assumed and in each such liberal judges as Stone and Brandeis and Cardozo agreed with their more conservative brethren. Furthermore, in the most important of them, the decision involving the National Industrial Recovery Act, it is highly significant that the judgment only slightly accelerated the demise of a statute which was about to expire anyway and which probably could not have been renewed.

These decisions nevertheless increased the tension between the administration and the Court. But far more important was the judgment of the Court in 1936 with regard to the Agricultural Adjustment Act. This case, *United States v. Butler,* turned on the constitutionality of a processing tax to be levied on certain products, the proceeds of this tax to be applied to provide subsidies for farmers who consented to limit acreage in accordance with a prescribed plan. The decision declared the so-called tax was not a tax, within the meaning of the Constitution, but a transfer of money from one group to another.

For several reasons the action of the Court aroused especial resentment. In the first place, the Court was divided six to three. In the second place, the decision nullified the efforts of the government to deal with the fundamental problem of agricultural prices and was followed by a severe price decline in the commodities affected. Robert Jackson, later a distinguished justice of the Court, wrote in 1941, some years after the event, "It is doubtful whether any judicial tribunal anywhere at any time has rendered a decision of such far-reaching and disastrous economic implications." Not only did the judgment of the Court fall heavily on the farming community, but it struck a serious blow at the federal finances, since it seemed to suggest that nearly a billion dollars collected in processing taxes would have to be refunded and, even worse than this, it would give those refunds in many instances to those who had passed on the tax itself to the consumer. And, finally, the decision produced one of the most passionate dissents in the history of the Court in the opinion of Mr. Justice Stone, a dissent which was bound to stimulate criticism already rampant.

Stone argued the impropriety of justifying "tortured construction of the Constitution" by citing "extreme examples of Congressional spending which . . . would be possible only by action of a legislature lost to all sense of public responsibility. Such suppositions," he pointed out, were "addressed to the mind accustomed to believe that it is the business of courts to sit in judgment on the wisdom of legislative action. Courts," he went on, "are not the only agency of government that must be assumed to have capacity to govern. Congress and the courts both unhappily may falter or be mistaken in the performance of their constitutional duty. But interpretation of our great charter of government which proceeds on any assumption that the responsibility for the preservation of our institutions is the exclusive concern of any one of the three branches of government, or that it alone can save them from destruction is far more likely in the long run, 'to obliterate the constituent members' of 'an indestructible union of indestructible states' than the frank recognition that language, even of a constitution, may mean what it says; that the power to tax and spend includes the power to relieve a nation-wide economic maladjustment by conditional gifts of money."

The language of Justice Stone went far beyond what was necessary to a decision of the Butler case. It was, in effect, a severe commentary on the Court itself. When a

Supreme Court justice of high reputation used such language, it was easy to understand the attitude of the administration. The question of curbing the power of the judges was under consideration for some time before the election of 1936. But the President made no issue of the matter before he was safely, and indeed triumphantly, reelected in that year. Then on February 5, 1937, he sent a message to Congress in which he recommended that he be given authority to appoint a new justice whenever a sitting judge reached the age of seventy and failed to retire on full pay. He based his request not on the previous decisions of the Court or on the difficulties that arose from the undoubted rigidity of view on the part of four of the justices but on the alleged fact that the Court was behind in its work. He even went so far as to say that the Chief Justice and his colleagues had been forced by the sheer necessity of keeping up with its business to decline, without even an explanation, to hear 87 per cent of the cases presented to it by private litigants for review.

The President's proposal under any circumstances would have awakened wide opposition. While the Court had undoubtedly in certain instances impeded the policies of the New Deal, many persons doubted the intrinsic wisdom of these policies and minimized the gravity of the Court's interruption of the legislative process. But what was equally important, the President had proceeded in a thoroughly disingenuous manner to deal with an important problem. His presentation of his case was marked by that quality of deviousness which was an undeniable limitation of this undeniably great President of the United States.

Charles Evans Hughes was profoundly shocked by the President's proposal and in the forthcoming struggle played a very important role. At the very outset he was placed by Roosevelt's indirection in a position to strike a damaging blow at the administration's program.

The hearings on the bill were held towards the end of March. The leader of the opposition was Senator Burton K. Wheeler of Montana. Very early in the Court fight he sought the counsel of the Chief Justice. What occurred may best be described in Hughes's own words. "As the opponents of the bill were about to present their case, Senators Wheeler, King and Austin called upon me — I think it was on Thursday, March 18th, 1937 — and asked me to appear before the Committee. I was entirely willing to do this for the purpose of giving the facts as to the work of the Court. Even in appearing for such a purpose, however, I thought it inadvisable, in view of the delicacy of the situation, that I should appear alone. It seemed to me that at least one other member of the Court should accompany me — preferably Judge Brandeis — because of his standing as a Democrat and his reputation as a liberal judge.

"I so informed the Committee. But when I consulted Judge Brandeis I found that he was strongly opposed to my appearing — or to any Justice appearing — before the Committee. I stated the desire of the Committee to have the facts as to the state of the work of the Court and suggested that I might, in response to a request, write a letter for that purpose. With that suggestion Justice Brandeis fully agreed. I found that Justice Van Devanter took the same view. . . .

"Later on Saturday, as I recall it — Senator Wheeler, who I understood had seen Justice Brandeis in the interval, called on me and asked me to write such a letter. He said that the Committee desired this letter so that it could be used on Monday morning at the opening of the hearing on behalf of the opponents of the bill. This gave me very limited time but I proceeded at once to assemble the necessary data, and on Sunday, March 21st, the letter was completed. I at once took it to Justice Brandeis and to Justice Van Devanter, and each went over it carefully and approved it."

Insofar as this letter was an answer to the President's charge that the Court was not abreast of its work the Hughes reply was absolutely devastating. The Chief Justice pointed out that when the Court had risen on March 15, it had heard argument on cases which it had accepted for review only four weeks before. He indicated, what was undeniable, that many applications for review involved no question of public interest sufficient to justify such action. "I think it is the view of the members of the Court that if any error is being made in dealing with these applications it is on the side of liberality. An increase in the number of Justices of the Supreme Court, apart from any question of policy, which I do not discuss, would not promote the efficiency of the Court. . . . There would be more judges to hear, more judges to confer, more judges to discuss, more judges to be convinced and to decide. The present number of Justices is thought to be large enough so far as the prompt, adequate, and efficient conduct of the work of the Court is concerned."

Despite its force the Hughes letter has come under severe criticism from a highly reputable source. Justice Stone was distinctly chagrined that more justices were not consulted before it was sent. He was of the opinion that some of them were easily available, not very far from Hughes's home, and that they could have been reached by telephone. And he disliked very much one sentence of the letter, a sentence not quoted above, in which the Chief Justice expressed the opinion that a suggestion of the President — that the enlarged Court should hear cases in divisions — was unconstitutional. In his view it was an impropriety for a Supreme Court justice to express an opinion on the constitutionality of a given proposal until it came before the Court in a regular way for review. There is, I think, some ground for these criticisms. But they are far from going to the central issue and they should not be given an exaggerated importance.

One week after the Hughes letter the Court reversed itself on the issue of the minimum wage. The Tipaldo case, it will be remembered, had declared a minimum-wage law unconstitutional by the close vote of five to four. Now, in the case of *West Coast Hotel v. Parrish,* the Court declared a similar act valid. Hughes himself delivered the opinion of the Court, and there was a ring of triumph in his voice as he did so. He had been on the same side since the beginning. It was Justice Roberts who now made possible the shift. And the shift in this case was only prelude. It foreshadowed such a change in the attitude of the Court as to make the Roosevelt proposal less and less necessary and less and less acceptable.

The decision in the case of *West Coast Hotel v. Parrish* was arrived at before the President's message to Congress; on this point we have the explicit assurance of the Chief Justice himself. But what produced Roberts's conversion? Since judicial conferences are strictly secret, it is possible that we shall never know. Was it due to the Chief Justice? Hughes's intimate biographer says that when Roberts "in a private chat" announced he would vote for sustaining the law, the Chief Justice "almost hugged him." Was this "private chat" where the conversion took place? We cannot answer this question. But it does not seem unreasonable to believe that in these early months of 1937, Hughes was laboring vigorously to bring his colleague to a view of the law more consonant with the undoubted drift of public opinion and with the social forces behind that opinion.

One week later the Court handed down its decision on the Wagner Act, a decision of profound significance not only in American constitutional law, but also in immediate political impact. It cut the ground from under the proponents of the President's proposal. It made it clear that a majority of the Court, narrow though this majority was, was prepared to accept the legal implications of the new climate of opinion. It placed the Court on the side of social adjustment, not of social rigidity.

Here again we cannot measure the forces that were operating in the chambers of the justices. Hughes's opinion in this case was by no means inconsistent with much of his previous judicial thinking. But what of Justice Roberts? Hughes himself says that Roberts was in no way influenced by the President's proposal. But it is difficult to prove a negative. We must therefore accept the Chief Justice's statement *cum grano*. And it leaves unanswered the question as to whether or not, within the framework of legal thinking, Hughes contributed, or how much he contributed, to the formation of the views of his colleague.

The decision on the Wagner Act was followed by other events which shook the President's program. On May 18 the Senate Judiciary Committee rejected the bill. A few days later the Supreme Court sustained the Social Security Acts, upholding legislation which provided for unemployment insurance and for old-age benefits. And in June came another, and in a sense a culminating, move. Justice Van Devanter resigned, and the President was thus given a chance to appoint a justice in his place. He chose Senator Hugo Black of Alabama, well known for his liberal views. Thus the ranks of the four conservatives on the bench were broken up. The balance of power on the Court had clearly shifted. By the middle of the summer it was clear that the Roosevelt project was no longer acceptable. The reorganization scheme had been defeated.

Divorced from the emotional heat of the moment, the issues of the great political struggle of 1937 seem clearer in retrospect. Looking backward, one can see that it was better that the President's plan be defeated, provided the Court showed itself capable of adjusting to the spirit of the times.

Hughes appreciated the character of the problem. His dislike of the court-packing plan did not throw him into the camp of the reaction. On the contrary, in the Wagner Act case he took ground more advanced than that which led him to go with the majority on the labor provisions of the coal cases. And the ring of triumph in his voice the day that the minimum-wage case was decided was ample evidence of the trend of his thinking. The Chief Justice was not aligned with the reactionary four.

Hughes himself vigorously denies in his autobiographical notes that the President's message produced the shift in the Court. He points out that the decision in the minimum-wage case had been settled before Roosevelt took the offensive against the tribunal. He asserts categorically (perhaps too categorically, since here he is reading another man's mind) that Justice Roberts's shift on the Wagner Act was in no sense induced by the court-packing plan. And he certainly implies that he himself was not influenced by the threat to the integrity of the bench.

However this may be, Hughes's service as Chief Justice after 1937 offers interesting evidence of his general attitude. In this period the composition of the Court was changed. Justice Van Devanter had resigned in June of 1937; he was soon to be followed by Justice Sutherland. Justice Butler died in 1939. The new appointees to the Court were in no instance of the cast of mind of their conservative predecessors. Hughes was destined, in his last years on the bench, to preside over a Court very different from the one to which he had come in 1930. In the shift in judicial construction that was evident there was nothing which caused him either pain or embarrassment. He was never found in dissent in cases involving the statutory policies of the New Deal. Against the sit-down strikes he delivered a vigorous opinion in 1939. But here he spoke for a unanimous Court. Some of his great decisions in the area of freedom of speech and of assembly came in these years. And in the new Court, as in the old, he had not only the affection but the respect of his colleagues.

But there was no doubt that he was aging. In his book on the Supreme Court, published in 1928, he had given a kind of halfhearted support to the idea that judges should be required to retire at the age of seventy-five. He was seventy-seven before signs of physical decline became really clear. Still, he hesitated. Then in 1941 he sent his resignation to the President. Amidst a chorus of praise he laid down his office.

He had left his mark deep upon the fabric of our constitutional law. He had contributed in an important way to the protection of civil liberties and the rights of minorities. He had played a part in the extension of governmental power through the commerce clause. He had helped to broaden the sphere of effective legislative action in the social and economic field on the part of the states. He had done something to "judicialize" the role of administrative bodies. In such cases as the Scottsboro case, he had put the interests of human beings above procedural considerations. He had, in his own person, given dignity to the judicial process.

He was not beyond criticism. There was sometimes a semantic element in his judicial decisions. His respect for precedent sometimes led him into a kind of logic-chopping. And while in constitutional matters he frequently took the broad view, he was sometimes charged with ultraconservatism in lesser matters. But we err if we seek to judge by a process of overrefined analysis. It is the large picture that stands. And that large picture shows us one of the few very great Chief Justices of the United States.

Epilogue

It remains in this brief biography only to summarize the place of Charles Evans Hughes in the story of American life.

Hughes grew to manhood, and even to early middle age, in a conservative period of American history. His Republicanism was the product of this era. He was untouched by the first wave of revolt that had its expression in the Populist movement and the free-silver campaign. Indeed, these phenomena only consolidated his party loyalty.

But he was touched by the reforming temper of the era of Theodore Roosevelt. His sense of the public interest, his dislike of financial dishonesty, his instinct for the popular mood, all made him a liberal governor of New York, a governor who was among the first to apply the principle of regulation to important business interests and to contest the power of a hard-bitten and reactionary political machine. And in the liberal policies of this epoch he combined zeal for reform with a remarkably highly developed administrative instinct. On the bench in his first term of service he identified himself with the nationalist tendencies of the time and with a growing reluctance to hamper social progress with the judicial veto. He was then, as always, a champion of civil liberty and of racial tolerance.

He went back into politics not because he disapproved of the Wilsonian domestic policies but because he saw, or thought he saw, that the foreign policy of the nation was inadequate to the challenge presented to it. Undoubtedly he found the policy of the administration weak and ineffective. But he could not formulate a positive policy of his own and he was caught between conflicting forces, between the strong desire of the American people for peace and the rising tide of sentiment in the East in favor of more vigorous action. He was at his least effective in the campaign of 1916. Nor can we entirely applaud his attitude in 1920. It may be that collective security is an iridescent dream. But, in the perspective that we have today, common action with other powers in the interests of peace is very much in the interest of the United States. Hughes was not opposed to the League of Nations, but he saw the problem of American participation in international organization from a limited, rather than from a far-sighted, point of view. In this, it must be candidly conceded, he reflected the prevailing sentiment of the American people.

Hughes was certainly one of the most distinguished American Secretaries of State. He grappled with a variety of problems effectively. He was brilliant in his handling of the Washington conference. He was effective, in his own day at least, in dealing with the reparations problem. He was forward-looking in his attitude towards Latin America. He does not, however, stand with that small number of statesmen who sowed great ideas in the public mind, ideas destined to grow and exert an influence over the decades. Even in the case of the good-neighbor policy, where he was to identify himself with the future, he was too much tied to the past to renounce completely for the United States that supervisory role which was to become more and more irksome to our southern neighbors.

As Chief Justice of the United States he stood in the very highest rank. In perspective he will be found among those who most clearly understood the role of judicial statesmanship and who attached the deepest and finest significance to the libertarian tradition where it was most important.

There has been ample evidence in this study of Hughes's independence in politics, of his devotion to the public good, of his high qualities of statesmanship. As a human being he was among the most extraordinary figures of his epoch. In intellectual power he stood in the first rank, at any rate in those fields in which he allowed his powers full play. In his standards of honor and fidelity to trust he was among the most scrupulous of men. He was not one who gave deep affection freely and, though he decidedly unbent as he grew older, he reserved his inner warmth for only a few. But in his family he was gay as well as devoted. At times he seemed a bit complacent. But his standards for himself were exacting, and only rarely did he fall away from them. It is easy for the scholar to take his scalpel and dissect, but it is more important to understand and to appreciate a great man when he appears. His own generation paid ample tribute to Hughes, and this is one measure of his stature. Other generations, which have lost the flavor of his personality and the impact of his virile and well-disciplined mind, will still find in him, when they know him, one of the great figures of American history.

A Note on the Sources

CHARLES EVANS HUGHES was extremely conscious of the claims of posterity and concerned with the proper evaluation of his own role. His papers in the Library of Congress cover his whole life, are remarkably well arranged, and with many of the folders goes a memorandum prepared by his secretary, Henry C. Beerits, summarizing the contents. His autobiographical notes are of great value and not only give an excellent outline of his life but reveal the points at which he was most sensitive to criticism. There exist, also, some excellent collections of his speeches. For the period of the governorship and for campaign addresses, see *Addresses and Papers of Charles Evans Hughes, 1906–1916,* revised, with new material including the speech of acceptance (New York, 1916). For the period of Hughes's Secretaryship, the best collection is C. E. Hughes, *The Pathway of Peace* (New York, 1925). There are two sets of lectures, *Our Relations to the Nations of the Western Hemisphere* (Princeton, 1928) and *Pan-American Peace Plans* (New Haven, 1929). For light on Hughes's philosophy of government, see his *Conditions of Progress in Democratic Government* (New Haven, 1910), and for his own views on the Supreme Court, his lectures, *The Supreme Court of the United States: its foundation, methods and achievements, an interpretation* (New York, 1928). His speeches in the campaign of 1916 and during the League fight are most conveniently found in the *New York Times.*

There is a large-scale biography of Hughes written by Merlo J. Pusey, who had the advantage of intimate contact with the Justice (*Charles Evans Hughes,* 2 volumes. New York, 1951). Pusey deals candidly with his subject but, perhaps inevitably, sometimes overstates his case.

There is no specialized study of Hughes as governor. But for his work on the Court there are two books. The older, W. L. Ransom's *Charles E. Hughes, the statesman as shown in the opinions of the jurist* (New York, 1916), is highly eulogistic and deals only with the Associate Justice. The more recent book by Samuel Hendel, *Charles Evans Hughes and the Supreme Court,* is a highly judicious work which is almost indispensable to an understanding of Hughes as a judge (New York, 1951). For a penetrating and critical view of Hughes on the Court, there is an important article by Alpheus T. Mason in the *Vanderbilt Law Review* (Volume VI, No. 1. December 1952), "Charles Evans Hughes: An Appeal to the Bar of History." See also by the same author *The Supreme Court: Vehicle of Revealed Truth or Power Group, 1930–1937* (Boston, 1953). A still more critical judgment, reflecting the passions of the time, is to be found in Irving Brant's two articles in the *New Republic* for July 1937. There is, of course, an immense literature on the Supreme Court fight in 1937, but any student of the problem should read Robert H. Jackson's *The Struggle for Judicial Supremacy, a Study of a Crisis in American Power Politics* (New York, 1941).

For the period of the Secretaryship the best source is the series *Foreign Relations of the United States* (publications of the United States Department of State). The materials for the years 1921–1925 in this important series are voluminous. There is an excellent analysis of Hughes by an admirer in the series known as *The American Secretaries of State and their Diplomacy* (New York, 1927–1929), edited by Samuel F. Bemis, Volume X. Hyde, the author of this sketch, had access to materials not then published. A more recent analysis, using both the published and the unpublished materials, is by the author of this volume in *The Diplomats* (Princeton, 1953). For the Far Eastern policy of this period the best brief account is in A. W. Griswold, *The Far Eastern Policy of the United States* (New York, 1938). For Latin America, see Samuel F. Bemis, *The Latin-American Policy of the United States, an historical interpretation* (New York, 1943). For Hughes's attitude towards the League, critically viewed, see Denna F. Fleming, *The United States and the League of Nations, 1918–1920* (New York, 1932).

What his own generation thought of Hughes is partially illustrated in the addresses delivered before the Supreme Court after his death. The volume is entitled *Proceedings of the Bar and Officers of the Supreme Court of the United States*, November 4, 1949, and *Proceedings before the Supreme Court of the United States*, May 8, 1950, *In Memory of Charles Evans Hughes*. Another appreciation, by a distinguished law teacher, Zechariah Chafee, Jr., is to be found in the *Proceedings of the American Philosophical Society*, Volume 93, No. 3.

Index

Charles Evans Hughes is abbreviated CEH.

LaVergne, TN USA
23 October 2009
161740LV00001B/22/P

9 780313 204630